AN ENGLISH GARDEN
IN PROVENCE

AN ENGLISH GARDEN IN PROVENCE

Natasha Spender

Photographs by Stephen Spender and Jean-Marie del Moral

THE HARVILL PRESS
LONDON

Natasha Spender

Eye, gazelle, delicate wanderer
Drinker of horizon's fluid line

STEPHEN SPENDER, 'POEMS', 1933

for Natasha
with love from
Christopher 1972

Contents

Paul Cézanne, Mont Sainte-Victoire, c. *1886–7*

Discovering the Landscape

When I try to imagine a faultless love
Or the life to come, what I hear is the murmur
Of underground streams, what I see is a limestone landscape.
W. H. Auden, 'In Praise of Limestone', 1948

We discovered Provence quite late in life, Stephen, my husband, in his early fifties and I not far behind. Hitherto our only excursion into rural France had been a joint tour immediately after the war, when he lectured and I gave piano recitals. In the post-war shortages travel had been uncertain, petrol unobtainable, trains irregular, and for our only two Provençal days at Aix-en-Provence we had been delightfully carried in our host's donkey cart. He had taken us to Le Tholonet, where we had clambered up to the Château Noir, and seen the majestic Montagne Sainte-Victoire that we knew so well from Cézanne. In the harsh midday light, haloed by that same bough of pine Cézanne had painted, it had appeared a stern monument, yet a glistening phantom.

It was some 15 years later that the true voyage of discovery took place, this time motoring in a new car, and free from professional duties. From first setting foot in France in early June, the going was leisurely and spacious, in tune with the wide, slow-flowing rivers where we lingered – the Seine, the Eure, the Yonne, the Loire. The quiet views of fishermen sitting by dark, satin waters, their cigarette smoke floating upwards before the gently ruffled poplar trees, in some sense set the pace for our journey. At last we travelled south by the great river Rhône, arriving at dusk at Villeneuve-lès-Avignon. Our room there for our first night in Provence was high in a turret overlooking the reeds and willows of the river and its island, with the ghostly towers of Avignon's floodlit Palais des Papes beyond. In early nightfall it was a dreamy scene of Tennysonian calm, where 'an abbott on his ambling pad' would have caused us no surprise.

But Avignon was no Camelot, as we discovered the following morning, and after battling through traffic and pottering through churches we were happy to leave the turmoil of the city behind, and take to country roads. Having crossed the Rhône and loitered at midday by

*The small honey-coloured Romanesque church
of Saint-Gabriel stands overlooking what
was one of the busiest crossroads in Europe*

the Pont du Gard, we recrossed and entered the *département* of the Bouches-du-Rhône by way of Beaucaire and Tarascon, which face each other over the river which marks the frontier between the regions of Languedoc and Provence. Once east of the Rhône, the landscape changes from the flatter expanses of low *garrigue* to the west, around Remoulins, Uzès and Nîmes. After very few miles we were in the limestone crags and fruit orchards of the Alpilles, that east-west chain of mountains, small in size yet immense in scale, where the great, serried mass of the Alps, descending in undulations from Mont Blanc, makes its last modest assertion before falling into the Mediterranean Sea.

This fall is not immediate, for there lies to the south the wide flatland of the Crau and the Camargue, composed of thousands of tons of earth deposited annually through the ages by the Durance and the Rhône delta. It was only comparatively recently that it was drained from the unhealthy marshes which daunted all travellers on the Grand Tour. Yet the stone from the ancient quarries of Fontvieille and Les Baux is full of fossilized seashells, and one imagines the prehistoric lapping of the sea around the crags of the Alpilles.

Prehistoric it must have been, for Crusaders set sail with Saint Louis – King Louis IX – from what is now the inland town of Aigues-Mortes, though lying several miles south-west of the Alpilles, and even the Roman general Scipio moored his fleet, when failing to catch up with Hannibal, at Fos-sur-Mer. Both these towns are on the southern coastal edge of this wide alluvial plain of the Crau and the Camargue. Then, even further back in history, there are the funeral steles, reputedly of a prehistoric culture, which were found in the Camargue, and the Celto-Ligurian remains found in the Crau. However, the marshes and lagoons of the Camargue reaching to the foot of the Alpilles existed from prehistory until medieval times when the monks of Montmajour, on an outcrop of the Alpilles, used to take to their punts to visit nearby Arles. Indeed, only a decade ago, just below the Alpilles at Maussane, a large marshy *étang*, which appeared vast in the rainy season, was at last drained and reclaimed.

We first touched the Alpilles that day at their western tip, where the small Romanesque church of Saint-Gabriel stands, as if upon a sea-girt promontory. Its façade clearly contains the remains of ancient Roman columns, and its honey-coloured stone glows in the sunlight. It overlooks what in Roman times had been one of the busiest crossroads in Europe. Here was Ernaginum, the port on the edge of the marshes, served by the 'navy of Arles'. At this point the Via Aurelia, which followed the Mediterranean coast from Rome to Marseille (Massalia) and along the south side of the Alpilles to Nîmes, crossed the Via Domitia, which descended from the Alps above Turin, led along the north side of the Alpilles, and thence to Spain. During a three year wait for the arrival from the north of the barbarian hordes with which he was to do battle, the Roman general Marius, uncle of Julius Caesar, had spent the time building through the marshy plain dykes and canals which focused on Ernaginum. No trace now remains of this formerly thriving

Looking north, the house amid the orchards, tucked under the Alpilles

The landscape beyond the house with its frieze of sun-whitened rock

crossroads and port of the 'Fosses Mariennes', and yet the slope above, with its large slabs of stone hewn from the living rock in the now deserted Roman quarry, has that haunting desolation of a forgotten, civilized antiquity.

Looking back, I see that there are many reasons why, on that voyage, I should have been ripe for a love affair with the Alpilles. The imagination is so often transported, not only by, say, a Celto-Ligurian sanctuary (Les Caisses de Servannes), or by Roman towns (such as Glanum, Tericias, Aureille or Castrum de Aquaria, which is now the modern Eyguières), but also by less grand traces of an antique way of life – the little aqueduct near Fontvieille, where the water supply for Arles turned millwheels on the cliff to grind corn, or the shards which we sometimes pick up, washed out after rainfall, at some Roman sentinel's outpost on the escarpment near Maussane.

But first things first; prior to the love of ruins it is the limestone landscape which captivates one's imagination. I have always found granite forbidding, but the younger limestone fascinating. One can imagine that the limestone crags were hurled up from the enveloping earth, having been vigorously hewn into overlapping knife-edge forms by a subterranean Pluto. Having emerged into daylight they may lose their implacability and respond to the softening blandishments of wind and weather, the mineral becoming transformed into animal or vegetable. The Vallée des Baux abounds in limestone eagles poised for flight, or fastigiate tree-forms in stone. There within the steep declivity of the Val d'Enfer, as in homage to Dante it is called, the stone has weathered into phantasmagorical shapes and a deepish ochre-grey patina, which at all seasons gives it an air of brooding damnation. But seen from the top of the ridge above (reached by a dirt road giving access in case of forest fires), the rocks seem more benign and happily melded with the village, so that Les Baux appears like a mushroom growth upon its saucer of limestone plateau. Elsewhere in the Alpilles, under brilliant Provençal skies, the rocks appear to surge towards the ridge and to change hourly with the passage of the sun. From their etched clarity of the early morning, they pass to the chalk-white incandescence of midday, and then to the mellowing light copper burnish of sunset.

A love for the arid contours of limestone is fostered by love of the Italian trecento and quattrocento painters, whose works were so often devoted to themes of religious contemplation, or of hermitage and desert asceticism. Hitherto my only experience, in reality, of these rock formations had been in the English Peak District near Dovedale, where they are surrounded by meadows, grazing sheep and cattle, hedgerows, oaks and elms in verdant harmony. Thus, the Italian artists' treatment of the selfsame stone (as in, for instance, Duccio's *Maestà*) had always seemed to me a fanciful, imaginary landscape, created in order to intensify a portrayal of the religious spirit in travail in the wilderness. Even in Benozzo Gozzoli's more worldly picture of a jolly party of richly attired Magi journeying to Bethlehem, *Procession of the Magi*, with its happy peppering of the background with mop-headed trees and a hunting scene, the limestone had seemed to be a textural conceit, like linen-fold woodcarving. Yet it is remarkable how true to nature these grooved convolutions are. My first encounter with the Alpilles was to be a surprised recognition in the natural world of several long-loved images in art. It was with such religious pictures of wilderness hermitage in mind that, years later, we were to name our house in the Alpilles 'Mas Saint-Jérôme'.

Although we had instantly welcomed the idea of Saint Jerome in that landscape, the particular Renaissance image from which it originated could not for some time be found, although it had remained vivid in my visual memory. It was an Italian picture portraying him alone in a just such a parched rocky landscape, a romantic young hermit figure, dragging his coat. It had not occurred to me to wonder that no friendly lion appeared in my recurring image, nor books, nor bearded ancient scholar. A year or two later, as I was wandering in the National Gallery in Washington, there, suddenly, was my picture. It almost sprang off the wall to greet me, and was, I discovered, the Domenico Veneziano which Bernard Berenson's wife had, much to his distress, given to a young friend who had been kind to her. Of course, to my amused chagrin, the lithe young figure was not Saint Jerome, but Saint John in the desert. However, as we have grown old in this house the contemplative Jerome became ever more appropriate. Stephen consoled me with a small Rembrandt etching of Saint Jerome and his lion, which for some years presided over the chimneypiece and even now is fondly remembered. But having at last read Saint Jerome's life the compelling question recurs: how could such a stern, repressive puritan have persuaded a lion to live in amity with him in the harsh desert?

Domenico Veneziano,
Saint John in the Desert, c. *1450*

Duccio di Buoninsegna, Noli Me Tangere,
detail of the Maestà Alterpiece, *1308–11*

The Chapelle de Saint-Sixte near Eygalières,
from which one approaches the Alpilles

The chain of the Alpilles is far from being a desert, however. Not only its dramatic sky-line shapes but also its colours, the grey-green olive trees, the cinnamon red earth and the inky black-green cypresses are inevitably exotic to a northerner's eyes. Just below the rocks, as well as *maquis* and *pinède*, there flourish the great orchards of apricot, almond, cherry or olive, the vineyards, and the fields of corn, lavender or sunflowers. In some ways agriculture has changed the *paysage* remarkably little since its introduction in ancient days, when the whole region had previously been covered in forests. The olive was brought to Provence in about 600 BC by the earliest Greek colonizers whose prince, Protis, had acquired as dowry Mas Salia (Marseille) when he married the daughter of the Segobrigian king. The Greeks also introduced the systematic culture of the vine, and in all probability apricots and more cultivated varieties of cherries, figs and chestnuts. Cornfields and almond trees would also have flourished in those times, and it is only more recently that they seem gradually to have yielded place to apricots, melons or vines. A decade ago in our valley there was a charming almond orchard underplanted with corn. It was radiant silver-pink in earliest spring, and its golden tone of high summer was punctuated by the eccentric black trunks of the almond trees. Now it has disappeared into the huge vineyard of the Mas Gourgonnier.

This landscape marriage of the arid with the fertile gave us another joyful recognition, the instant evocation of Van Gogh. Here again, I had always assumed his vision of swirling cypresses to have sprung from his instability of mind. Yet on that first day of our tour I saw their crazed turbulence in a strong mistral, that wind which, from the Alps, races in gathering anger down the funnel of the Rhône valley. He had painted no more than the truth, as indeed we discovered further when staying the second night in Saint-Rémy-de-Provence. We contemplated the odd, knobbly profile of Les Alpilles, which forms the background of so many works he painted there, when living in the little asylum of the Cloître de Saint-Paul-de-Mausole. Having once seen the dramatic line of Mont-Gaussier and Les Deux Trous (the rock with two holes in it), one can never again see his *Olive Trees* with the Alpilles in the background as deranged expressionism, though at each revisiting of the site, his forceful veracity lives always in one's mind.

After a few more days of our gentle explorations, I, for one, was completely hooked. In that time we had wandered over nearly every road in these mountains west of Salon-de-Provence. Approaching them from the more distant Cavaillon in the Vaucluse to the north (and now from the *autoroute*, non-existent in those days), the Alpilles have a jagged aspect which makes them seem much larger, more monumental and more distant – more truly Alpine – than they are. Then as one drives toward them, from the little Chapelle de Saint-Sixte, they begin to assume a quite Wagnerian drama. And from the Eygalières-to-Mouriès road, which passes right through them, they seem to loom towards one with momentary menace, before regaining their rugged repose behind the spreading vineyards of the Vallonge. From there to the hamlet of Le Destet, the Mouriès road winds down through pinewoods, yellow scented broom, and sometimes bizarre outcrops of rock, a

Benozzo Gozzoli, The Journey of the Magi to Bethlehem, *c. 1460*

delicately changing scene which reminds one of a Chinese scroll painting, or of some corners of Kyoto. From Le Destet turning west towards Maussane there is a high valley of great beauty at the heart of the Alpilles, known somewhat floridly by the older inhabitants as the 'Val des Amants'.

When we had tried all the 'roads not adopted and woodlanded ways', it was to this almost concealed high valley that we often returned. We particularly fell in love with a small ruined farmhouse amongst the rocks, and with a distant view of Arles. Setting out from Maussane and branching eastward into the mountain, the 'Route du Destet' approaches that little house by three steeply ascending corkscrew turns, before it reaches the narrow stretch of apricot and olive orchards surrounded by pinewoods, and beyond them the gleaming rocky ridges of limestone. The *maquis* had encroached to the walls of the ruin, uninhabited as it had been for many decades. There we picnicked almost daily, sitting in its shade, surrounded by rosemary, thyme and juniper, humming with insect life. Somewhere in the vicinity there were beehives, and indeed, Miel des Alpilles is one of the local delicacies which we often carry back to London. Occasionally a battered van would pass, bearing farmworkers to their tasks, and in the long afternoon we would hear, faintly, their laughing chatter from the fields beyond. Those were days of enchanted timelessness.

During the next three or four years, whenever we drove south, often to Italy, we would allow time to make a detour pilgrimage to what we had now come to think of as 'our ruin'. We had enquired in the village of Maussane whether it could be for sale. But the intricate consequences of the *Code Napoléon* were explained to us, whereby in law next-generation heirs must benefit equally, and thus properties are carved into smaller and smaller segments with each succession. This particular little farm was the subject of some confusion between the many owners, and we were advised not to pursue it. As it transpired this was fortunate for us, since although others have now successfully reunited and restored it, its proximity to the road and lack of garden space have long since diminished its attraction for us as a potential home. Nevertheless, its charm as a landmark is perennial.

It must have been four years after our first discovery of the Alpilles that, in the

Vincent van Gogh, The Olive Trees, *1889*

The olive grove beyond the house on the way to the canal, by the little road that leads to Mouriès

lull between his attending Westminster School and New College, our son Matthew with our future daughter-in-law Maro, both painters, spent six months at Cézanne's Château Noir at Le Tholonet, which had been converted into artists' studios. At Easter we went with our daughter, Lizzie, to spend some part of the holidays near them, staying at an hotel overlooking Picasso's Château de Vauvenargues, in the valley just north of the Montagne Sainte-Victoire.

On impulse one day when, unusually, everyone of the party seemed a shade desultory, I suggested taking a picnic to 'our ruin', some 40 miles away in the Alpilles. During the journey of an hour or so, I made the mistake of describing the place with highly lyrical abandon, going quite 'over the top' in enthusiastic anticipation, so as to kindle the spirits of the family. Mistake it certainly turned out to have been, for since Stephen and I had paid it a visit in the previous year, there had been a forest fire. All that remained of that scented tapestry of *maquis* and *pinède* were some charred tree stumps and acres of soil blackened with ash, through which a few sprouting clumps of fresh green foliage were struggling to emerge. Matthew, at that time passing through a short phase of adolescent censoriousness, remarked, 'Typical of you to like something so austere', as we drove on in dazed disappointment, Stephen and I continuing vainly the attempt to describe its former glory.

But almost immediately Matthew pointed cheerfully and dramatically south at the rocks beyond a fluttering olive orchard, silver-grey in the breeze, and persuaded us that THERE lay the most beautiful picnic site imaginable. Indeed it was. No sign here of incendiary devastation, all was burgeoning. There were some apricots and wild cherries in bloom on the brink of a little valley, where the silky sheen of the tops of olive trees showed in the terraced field below the abandoned vineyard in which we stood. At our feet, among the dead vines, was a sprinkling of wild flowers in great variety, among them tiny marigolds, marguerites, flax and early poppies. We gazed beyond olives and pines at the spectacular range of mountain rocks laid out against the sky. Turning, we saw in the stony, bedraggled field behind us another ruined farmhouse, this one open to the four winds, and darkly enveloped in ivy. The children became exuberant and climbed all over it, while we continued to contemplate with pleasure the sloping, wild terrain, with its frieze of sun-whitened limestone.

Inside the crumbling walls of the ruin, large scruffy trees were growing, and a solitary decaying wooden beam, log-shaped, hung half its length between end walls, high above the ground. At one corner there was a stone trough which had clearly been used as a manger in what was evidently the *bergerie* attached to the little house. (Later we were told that it was probably a sarcophagus since its oblong shape was characteristically wider at one end.) Outside the *bergerie* was a stone lean-to pen, apparently for goats, and a ruined well, dry as far as we could see, and overgrown with a tangled bush of figs. Inside the house, a few steps of an old stone staircase ended in mid-air. The whole forsaken scene seemed arrested in a time some decades earlier. After these explorations we found the perfect spot

On the rocks, our house on the left, and Matthew on the ruin the day we discovered it

The ruin in 1965, uninhabited since World War I, soon to be named Mas Saint-Jérôme

under the pine trees in which to lay out our feast and gather round it. The magic of the day had been retrieved, our picnic in the lazy afternoon a happy one.

Our affection for the 'Val des Amants' soon became focused anew. The ruin originally discovered on the edge of the steeply winding Route du Destet became in our minds only a kind of prelude to the new and more welcoming vista leading to our recent picnic place. The thoughts of its fascination often returned, but we went away and thought of other landscapes, too.

A few weeks later, when motoring alone towards England, I paused to have tea with some English friends who had settled at the Mas des Imberlines, which stands back on flat land just south of the Maussane-to-Mouriès road. She was a translator and he a writer on evolutionary humanism, of evangelical disposition, who for his living was also farming melons. They had restored adjoining houses. Hers was charming, elegant and comfortable, its furniture and its colours enhancing the impression she herself gave, of a beautiful woman who valued wellbeing and composure. His house was stark, its contents pared to improvised basics, as was his dress and appearance. His intense pale blue eyes flashed from bony features; he was tall, blond and lean, clad in minimal shorts, raw leather sandals and a rough cotton shirt. They were each of them in different ways knowledgeable about the locality, and justly proud of having found their place in the community, pioneering its restoration from partial decay by the strangers who increasingly came and found they wished to live there.

Having heard from them an account of their respective transformations of the *mas*, I asked rather tentatively whether there were now any ruins for sale. She replied with friendly exasperation, 'Oh, why didn't you ask me two years ago? There were such attractive ones then. Now they have all gone.' He meanwhile was looking increasingly stern and, leaning his ascetic face toward me, said earnestly, 'Do you REALLY MEAN it? After all, it's a WAY of LIFE.' His way of life being a day timetabled with military precision, and divided between early morning melon farming, and sitting writing at a bare stone table outside his front door, under a slatted *canisse* awning, grappling with ideas of evolutionary humanism, I began to feel a little uncertain whether I really did mean it. So I rather quickly changed the subject to more frivolous interests I shared with her; and I believe this evaporation of the high moral tone caused him to leave, abandoning us to our gossip. When, after a pleasant hour, I rose to resume my journey, she said, as if suddenly remembering, 'Oh yes, there is just one ruin for sale,' although she seemed doubtful whether it would be of interest. But I had an instant upsurge of enthusiasm, impatience even, to see it there and then. She told me nothing further about its location. But she gave directions as we drove over the most minor of dirt roads up into the mountain. A few more turnings, through olive orchards and over the agricultural canal, past peaks of eroded limestone, through pinewoods, and we had arrived. I could scarcely believe it, for it was the very ruin over which the children had clambered on our picnic day. Behind it in the next field stood another ruin, larger and even more weighed down by ivy and trees gone wild, but that, she said, was not available.

Clearly, it was meant for us. I stood there, calmly recognizing that it was to be ours. There were no doubts, questions or hesitations, save only a prudent concern for an adequate source of water, since it was three miles from the village, and thus out of range of the communal supply. We summoned the local builder on the following day, and the excellent Monsieur Lopez looked it over appraisingly, searched the tangle of suckers round the old stump of a fig tree and examined the well beneath. It had, he said, provided water for 'Sixteen people from both ruins, and ten great beasts' (oxen, I wondered?), so it was thought to promise more than enough for us. The house had been uninhabited since the First World War, he told us, and during the Occupation by the Germans in 1943 it had been used for target practice, having been fired at from the rocks above. This accounted for its pockmarked crumbling walls and the gaping holes in them. Although it looked so battered and friendless, Monsieur Lopez had an evident affection for it, and a desire to see it regain its perfect health.

Within a month we had bought it, and the odd little field in which it stood. Matthew immediately talked of it as 'Mother's Ruin', though for us from the first moment it was 'Mas Saint-Jérôme'. There was a startled moment in the lawyer's office when the *Acte de Vente* was read aloud, and heard to contain an unexpected clause reserving for a neighbouring farmer a *droit de puisage*. This meant that he, and his, could come and help themselves to drinking water from our well, entering the property by any route designated by us, although he could not take water for his crops. This evoked in us a twinge of anxiety, but perhaps, we thought, he might never avail himself of the right.

This is the only house I have ever owned, and the only country garden I have made. There was an atavistic pleasure in feeling the earth under our feet to be, as it were, a sure – and I hoped fertile – foundation for the life that our family would lead there, and our realization of that was an emotional moment. That earth would be cared for with devotion, and would burgeon in due season. Our land was to be a harmony of colours and forms within the tiered folds of landscape which seemed to enclose it like encircling arms, the rocks, the pines, the olives – and then, the garden. Visions of a mini-Mediterranean Sissinghurst crowded my thoughts. I saw it all in my mind's eye, though at that moment I was gazing at a few dead vines in an almost barren field of chalk-pale earth, an anaemic-looking marl. I reverently filled a small plastic bag with my very own soil, and took it to the Royal Horticultural Society in London to be analysed. Back came the report that it was quite the poorest soil which they had ever analysed.

My education in Provençal gardening had begun.

Limestone crags in the etched clarity of morning light with distant Caisses de Servannes (left) and flatlands of the Crau beyond

The encircling rocks, pines and olives seen looking south from Stephen's study

CHAPTER 2

Dreams and Design

We get snatches of divine loneliness here; [. . .] thank the Lord, we shall be alone;
we'll play bowls; then I shall read Sévigné; then have grilled ham and
mushroom for dinner; then Mozart and why not stay here for ever and ever,
enjoying this immortal rhythm, in which both eye and soul are at rest?

VIRGINIA WOOLF TO VANESSA BELL, 'LETTERS', 8 OCTOBER 1938

There never had been such a landscape in my earlier memory, and none of the English gardens I had known well would have married into it. Parched and stony earth beneath the silvery olives, and darkest pines before the skyline surge of rocks felt a thousand miles from the velvet green valleys and deciduous trees of my former experience. It was a year before I had taken it into my mind so far as to be able to conjure at will the image of its every etched line and texture. This was the year of sporadic visits, in order to direct or cajole the workmen into rebuilding the ruin as I had designed it to be. At times this was an all-consuming struggle, to which any thought of cultivating the arid plot had to yield to second place. But the garden dream went on. No one embarking on such a project could have had less experience than I, nor less knowledge of the climate and natural habitat, nor yet a head more teeming with ambitious imaginings. My happy store of remembered impressions of English gardens, though resisting attempts to visualize their many virtues translated into this wild landscape, included two in which I had lived over many years, Funtington and Bruern, and three, Monk's House, Sissinghurst and Hidcote, which I had often lovingly visited.

Throughout childhood, and later as a music student, I had spent long idyllic weeks at the home in West Sussex of George and Margy Booth and their family of six children, great friends of my mother and myself. Funtington Lodge was a seventeenth-century house which had been extended in rather zig-zag fashion in successive centuries. The garden had correspondingly many corners to be turned, with unexpected visual pleasures as one made one's way round them from the old house to the newest addition, the music room, for this was a family of musicians. Aunt Margy (as I knew her), carrying her violin case over to the music room, could be seen pausing here and there on her walk, at certain plants, as if to give them affectionate encouragement. To this day, the scent of lavender or 'cherry pie' (heliotrope) evokes in me an echoed memory – sounds of practising coming from different bedrooms, or the concerted vitality of string quartets pulsing from the open windows of the music room.

I was perhaps six years old when the Booths acquired 'Funty', and my earliest garden memory is of an ancient medlar tree, and a huge Spanish chestnut in the branches of which the children, all older than I, had a wooden tree-house. The joy was to be allowed to join them there among the dark foliage, pulling the ladder up after us, impregnable in our leafy hideaway. As soon as she had taken possession of Funtington Lodge, Aunt Margy had immediately planted a catalpa. Its boughs after a few years were almost sweeping the ground, so that here was another paler green canopy and favourite haunt of play. Today, more than seventy years later, I see in my long-standing garden notebook a numbered list of desires for trees and shrubs, some unfulfilled. There, still at the top of the list is *Catalpa bignonioides*. Alas, until we can extend the garden, we would have no place for it. But at Mas Saint-Jérôme other childhood memories of 'Funty' are revived and affections accommodated in the opulent pure white poppies of *Romneya coulteri*, and a wine-dark *Clematis* 'Ville de Lyon'. Most loved of all were the blood-red wallflowers within their box hedges, both of which scented the air as one arrived at the front door, in excited anticipation of yet another glorious holiday.

The charm of the Funtington garden was in its character as a series of linked, almost cottage gardens, beautifully planted and well chosen, with the style more of a cadenza than of a sonata movement. The central themes were there, but informally. Each plant was loved for its intrinsic character. Whether it was rare or fashionable was entirely immaterial; that was never a consideration. Nor were shrubs consciously placed as a 'feature', as is so often the taste of today. Aunt Margy had herself grown up in Victorian times, living before her marriage at Mottisfont Abbey in Hampshire, with its long lawns gently sloping to the river Test, its great cedar tree and towering walls clad with *Magnolia grandiflora*. (Now that it is a National Trust property, Graham Stuart Thomas has transformed the vast walled space of its former kitchen garden into a unique collection of old and newer roses.) Her particular talent was in scaling down a vision nurtured in Victorian grandeur to a simple episodic design, and in choosing plants and the places for them with unselfconscious flair.

Perhaps as patrons and friends of Vanessa Bell, Duncan Grant and other artists of the Omega Workshops, the Booths would have known well the various modest Bloomsbury gardens in East Sussex, yet Funtington had an original and distinctive personality. It was not simply a cottage-cum-kitchen garden, like that of Vanessa Bell at Charleston Farmhouse. It was larger and more differentiated, with its lily pond at one far corner, its sunken rose garden and (rare in the 1930s) its trefoil-shaped swimming pool. Apple trees and sweet peas in profusion lined the grassy paths of the kitchen garden, which was separated from the house by the driveway and garages, and which in character resembled

Aunt Margy and Uncle George at Funtington

Mottisfont Abbey on the river Test

From this crest one sees Arles, the sea and, in winter, the Montagne Sainte-Victoire

The ruin undergoing its various stages of reconstruction

a French *potager*. From there we would pass through a wicket gate and walk through a few fields up on to the windswept South Downs, without touching a road. The long family walks before lunch, surrounded by scampering rabbits, over turf springing with harebell, coltsfoot, speedwell and vetch, refreshed us for the music making of the afternoon. This formed my ideal of country living, to have free and natural access to the wild.

Here at Saint-Jérôme we walk through the garden straight up into the *pinède* and on, over anciently terraced slopes, to the crest of the rocks. At each step the view changes, and the house appears to nestle ever more cosily below, until at the summit we can see ridge upon ridge of the Alpilles, then Les Baux, Arles and the sea. Further still, on a fine winter's day, to the east we see the Montagne Sainte-Victoire 40 miles away, whilst equally far to the west there is the Massif Central and the Cévennes behind Nîmes.

Sixty years ago the atmosphere was not yet so polluted by sprays and insecticides as it has come to be. I remember Funtington as murmuring with bees and darting with butterflies. This has always remained in my memory as an image of country garden delight. At Saint-Jérôme we are at least fortunate to be so close to the wild, so that the insect life has more chance to survive than it can in the square miles of sprayed orchards and market gardens to the north of the Alpilles. This morning, at lilac time in late April, we have seen clouds of swallowtails, tortoiseshells and humming-bird hawkmoths besieging the flowering sage, whilst little white darlings with tiny black polka dots, and brilliant azure blue ones unidentifiable by me are finding the lilac irresistible.

The most bewitching yet serene of 'Bloomsbury' gardens was that of Monk's House, at Rodmell, in East Sussex, the home of Leonard and Virginia Woolf. I first saw it in 1941, a few weeks after her death, and we continued to visit Leonard there for nigh on thirty years.

Before we arrived on that sunny April day of my first visit – it must have been very soon after my marriage and twenty-second birthday – Stephen had been rebuking himself, as people so often do after a suicide, since he had received a letter from Virginia, and had delayed his response to her plea for 'an immensely long letter' for some days, until he would be able to include a new poem he was writing. Almost the last letter which she had written to a friend had been to Stephen; in the event his reply would have been too late, and quite unrelated to her state of mind.* But his remorse for his procrastination, perhaps understandably over-important to him in retrospect, was nevertheless as little, compared to the concern he felt for Leonard.

It was one of the most remarkable first meetings of my life. Leonard met us at the gate, a thin elderly man, his long, craggy face showing gentle kindliness, wisdom, and evoking the biblical beauty of a Romanesque figure. He led us up the brick path, through the small enclosed garden, then past the old apple trees under which spring bulbs glistened like innumerable lighted candles, till we found a resting place by the shallow pond. We sat there on the lawn, which was open to the view, looking out over the water meadows which seemed to merge with the garden, and further, over the valley of the river Ouse towards the

* This letter written on 7 March, 1941, (No. 3,587) will be correctly dated in future editions of the *Collected Letters*.

distant chalk bluffs of Mount Cabuin. Beside us a beautiful *Sorbus aria* (whitebeam) was coming into its chalky grey-green foliage, and the pale flowerbuds, each surrounded by its circle of leaves, were like candelabra. On that day it seemed an almost cruel annunciation of spring.

Whatever his inner anguish may have been, he told the story of Virginia's last days simply, with the stoicism of a Greek philosopher, the sensitivity of a devoted husband, and with acceptance and respect for her action in the face of impending, intolerable illness. His understanding and nobility were such as to quell, or at least help to resolve (as far as that is ever possible with a sudden death), the distress his hearers would feel for the loss of a radiantly creative and beloved friend.

Far from our thoughts as we listened, making us forget our surroundings, every contour of the garden impressed its image upon us. The garden seemed to reflect the qualities of each of its creators, and their mutuality. It shone with the quiet and joyful labour of love which had gone into its making. Most poignant of all was the closed door of the wooden 'garden-lodge' near the lawn's edge which, when Virginia had been engaged in writing, had been her retreat. Perhaps literary pilgrims still sense the extraordinary beauty that was there, though, sadly, the garden no longer lives as it once did.

On the many subsequent visits over the years, I came to know Leonard better, as friend and as gardener. He taught me so much, and seemed to be quite unconcerned with the depths of my ignorance, although he would laugh at my beginner's attitude with its urgent ardour for planting. I said then (now no longer true) that I found weeding a boring task. Surprised and gently smiling he said, 'Oh, but that's just an enjoyable discipline.' For his friends, the particular inspiration of his gardening personality was in his tender passion for helping plants to thrive, and his delight in the happy accidents of nature. I remember, on one of my visits, that a ten-week stock had seeded itself in one of his greenhouses. It proceeded to behave like Jack's beanstalk, growing a hard wooden trunk like an old climbing vine. His other elegant, recherché plants were successively ousted from their allotted places as it rampaged over benches, windows and the roof with a profusion of pale, orchid-pink blooms. Leonard welcomed and cherished this mad aberration of nature with indulgent amusement, as if he were contemplating the over-exuberant party behaviour of an otherwise demure and modest friend.

Of course, the 'Woolves' being such friends, and gardening friends, of Harold and Vita Nicolson, the garden at Monk's House was in some ways a first cousin of that at Sissinghurst, but as different from it as first cousins can be, though tenuously bound by family feeling. Admiring once a towering and fragrant balsam poplar at Monk's House, I asked Leonard where it had come from. 'Well actually,' he said, 'Harold brought it back from Morocco in his breast pocket.' The delight of discovering plants, taking cuttings, bringing them home, sharing them with friends, encouraging the plants to make their home with us like foster-children, is a pleasure shared by many gardeners. Such foundlings

Leonard Woolf at Monk's House in 1941, a few weeks after Virginia's death, sitting under the great chestnut tree, talking of recent times

*Stephen, Natasha and Leonard at Monk's
House beside the shallow pond.
Beyond are the water meadows, and the chalk
downs rising to Mount Cabuin*

became happy members of the garden family, both at Monk's House and at Sissinghurst. Nevertheless, in their social life the Nicolsons enjoyed both the simple intimacy of a few friends and the more formal, worldly entertaining, whereas the Woolves really enjoyed and sought only intimate, informal occasions. So, too, their gardens differed. Naturally size was a factor. But a large crowd of people visiting Monk's House would always have seemed incongruous with its style – intrusive or even disturbing – whereas the gardens at Sissinghurst seem to be giving serene yet high spirited welcome to large groups of garden lovers. The visitors' enjoyment is gracefully accommodated by some of its more formal vistas, with their air of finery and festivity.

Monk's House, however, gave of its best when one was in reflective mood, as a secret shared among friends, and among the visitors who came, two or three at a time, on the rare 'open' days. It had an unaffected purity of style, with here and there a touch of happy eccentricity. Some flowers, primroses or the starry *Tulipa tarda*, for instance, looked as if they had been tucked into a border for fun; they seemed to be winking at the world. The flowering quince would cheerfully hug its brick and grey flint wall with friendly glow, and a cactus in the greenhouse would assume an amusing knobbly stance, in apparent imitation of Leonard's figure when stooping to play *boules*.

Then, in sober contrast to the open, shallow pool at Monk's House, there was a small rectangular one enclosed by deeply shadowing yew hedges, its surface black as marble, through which slender water iris ascended, illuminating the dark secrecy of the scene. But all else in the garden was light and natural; roses jostling on the white weatherboarding of the house, or a crowd of cyclamen sunning themselves on the windowsill of the upstairs sitting room. There we would sit long over tea, enjoying conversation which I remember as serious without solemnity, as witty, quick and quiet, so much at one with the character of the garden.

Leonard disliked, as since my Funtington childhood I had done, over-neat, regimented gardens, containing impeccable, razor-sharp lawn edges, rectangular plots of roses or bedding plants and, surrounding the house, what one has come to think of as cliché shrubs. Now, half a century or so later, some of yesterday's strokes of wild originality are in danger of becoming today's clichés. For instance, the willow-leaved pear (*Pyrus salicifolia* 'Pendula') which Vita Sackville-West rediscovered and so imaginatively surrounded by the White Garden at Sissinghurst, enhanced an inspired composition. It has now become fairly ubiquitously used as a feature on tidy lawns, where it may be conceded a certain beauty in a breeze, but somehow looks a shade denuded and self-conscious. Taking a walk with Leonard in some downland village, he would stand on tiptoe to peer over the high wooden fence surrounding a substantial house. Then he would dismiss what he saw of the garden rather sniffily, his initial consonants sounding quite explosive. 'P-ublic P-ark', he would say, turning with relief towards a cottage garden, or to the fluid, timeless line of the Downs.

But he was discerning and generous in his praise for neighbouring gardeners who, as he did, devoted themselves affectionately to doing the best for many and unusual varieties of plants. He would attentively tour the various stands at the annual fête held by Lord Gage at Firle Place, looking as if he were at the Governor's garden party in Ceylon – a distinguished figure, wearing a Panama hat, white tussore jacket and immaculate tie adorned with shining tie-ring. Though not uncompetitive, he loved acknowledging others' successful exhibits or newly propagated varieties which he found attractive. If only I had then been better equipped to profit, as I now might do, from his expert observations and enthusiasms! Nevertheless, his guidance through the years was an inestimable bonus, which still remains with me.

He was fond of Provence, and in his eighty-ninth year had intended to visit us at Saint-Jérôme with our mutual friend, Peggy Ashcroft, but at the last moment the trip had to be cancelled because of unexpected practical difficulties. As Stephen and I were motoring home to London by way of Newhaven, we called at Monk's House bearing two plants of basil in ornate Italian terracotta pots, which he could overwinter in his greenhouse and savour through the bleaker months. We said that he MUST come and stay with us to enjoy a postponed Provençal interlude in the following year. He laughed appreciatively and, as a teasing joke, said, 'You AREN'T meaning to suggest that I shall be alive this time next year?' His vitality and fun were so striking that the suggestion was easily and robustly maintained by us. But we were mistaken. We were left with only gratitude for a wonderful friendship.

Stephen already knew Sissinghurst, in Kent, when he took me there on my first visit, also in 1941. Even though it must have already been suffering from wartime retrenchment, the garden appeared to flourish in generous and harmonious variety. During luncheon, when conversation had been almost entirely literary, Vita had seemed to me, young as I was, to be aloof and rather daunting. But later, strolling round the garden with an old tweed jacket flung over her fine cream silk shirt, her unapproachable calm was jettisoned as she suddenly made a dive to the ground, joyfully to uncover some tiny, jewel-bright flowers nearly hidden below foliage. Instantly, our reserve was melted by her affectionate gardening enthusiasms, and the stylized conversation of the earlier hour dissolved almost into chatter.

But the fun of discovering so many treasures small and great, which were both novel and beguiling, was only part of the impression I carried from that first visit. A greater impact was made by the whole notion of long vistas, where the sense of approaching a destination – a statue or a fountain – preserves in one's exploration a calm rhythm of purpose, within which the pleasures of individual plantings are enjoyed, not as a digression, but as the intrinsic theme in an onward movement. This theme is overtly evident in the formal Lime Walk, where symmetrically spaced pleached limes on either side are bordered by their long carpet of spring bulbs. But it is just as compelling in the more asymmetrical Moat Walk, which is backed on one side by a tree-and-shrub border, while the other has

At Sissinghurst in the company of Quentin Bell, Nigel Nicolson and Anne Olivier Bell

Sissinghurst, South Cottage and Stephen standing outside the Tower

a high and mellow Elizabethan brick wall of the former moat festooned with flowering shrubs and climbers.

It was here that I realized the importance, within a garden, of having these leafy ornamental 'corridors' as well as 'rooms'. To turn a corner and be led towards a distant view is an essential contrast to turning into an enclosed garden which will invite a more prolonged repose. These ideas, no doubt elementary to the seasoned gardener, I retained until there was a venture of my own. Although the garden proper at Saint-Jérôme is little more than an acre, we too have walks. Statuary would be too elegant and grand for our style and for our rugged landscape, so the modest destination of the Lilac Walk is simply a tall terracotta pot in Mycenaean style, copied for us by our friend David Plante from one in the British Museum.

In the summers of many years until 1994, more than 50 years since my first visit to Sissinghurst, we stayed for two weeks at South Cottage in the garden, as guests of our seasonally absent friends, Ed and Carol Victor. My rediscovery of the garden's beauties, particularly in the silence and mysterious light of dawn or dusk, has lifted my imagination on to another plane (for my dreams are forever running ahead, to extend our garden beyond the confines of the present plot). Now, with the experience I lacked in Vita's lifetime, I can more knowledgeably appreciate her superb sense of the characters – almost personalities – of plants, and of how happily they live within her architectural style. Her originality and faultless sense of plant and place have lived on, decades after her death, through the great creative gifts of the subsequent head gardeners, Pamela Schwerdt and Sybille Kreutzberger, and more recently their successor, Sarah Cook. A garden is not a museum, and to preserve and advance its traditional character through the vicissitudes of 'nature's changing course untrimmed' demands not only an accurate memory for how things were, but an imaginative eye for how newcomers will fit into the garden family. Sissinghurst is an all too rare example of the survival of a great garden, alive with the spirit of its origins, yet flexibly accommodating within its character the new generations of plants and the changes caused by unforeseeable buffetings of nature.

Visits to Sissinghurst were only sporadic over the years, as were those to Hidcote in Gloucestershire. Here was a garden principally of 'rooms', the main 'corridor' being a bare sward, unadorned, contained between high hornbeam hedges, and leading eventually to a Gainsborough meadow view of grazing cattle among spreading oak trees. One comes through each doorway cut in the hornbeam hedge to a fresh surprise, each room unique, with not a single theme repeated nor even echoed. On my visits there from nearby Oxfordshire I was to be dazzled, first by the perfection of each small garden, and then by the wealth and variety of plants as yet unfamiliar to me. Revisiting it after a great many years it continues to fascinate, and is even more crammed than before, though it is sad that the Gainsborough view has been superseded. Yet every visitor must find Hidcote an education in both gardening vocabulary and composition, which jogs one's inventiveness

David Plante and the Mycenaean pot he copied

into mentally composing gardens, much as one mentally composes letters to friends whilst waiting at a bus stop. Alas, in my case the letters seldom get written, but composing never ends in a garden. Moreover, of one's vocabulary of desirable plants, extended year by year, each clamours to be found a perfect niche, and many are left waiting. Thirty years after the joy of first seeing them at Hidcote, radiant on a dull November day, we at last have a group of the lovely 'Gruss an Aachen' roses, thanks to Peter Beales. Hidcote also teaches us the charm of the unexpected, as in passing from a cool and wild stream garden to a border designed to blaze with red and orange, or in the witty seeming accident of a minute strand of brilliant scarlet *Tropaeolum speciosum* creeper draping the severe architectural pediment on clipped 'walls' of darkest yew. Hidcote releases one from disenchantment into flights of gardening fancy.

However, ideas born in the exuberance of excursions into the high life of gardening can be a shade unruly until they have been brought to terms with the garden as the ambience of ones daily life. The garden at home must encourage not only the diffuse frivolous strollings of leisure but also the quiet, intense collecting of thoughts when one is immersed in creative work, be it writing or music.

By good fortune, a sustained influence on my gardener's eye came from our ten years spent in the Red Brick Cottage lent to us by Michael Astor in 1956, a Queen Anne dower house in his garden at Bruern Abbey. Until its destruction in the reign of Henry VIII the original Bruern had been a Cistercian abbey, though nothing of it now remains, save perhaps for a kind of Fra Angelico-vaulted ceiling in the Red Brick Cottage, and the fish pond fed by waters from the river Evenlode. Bruern is on the Oxfordshire edge of the Cotswolds near Shipton-under-Wychwood. The imposing classical façade of the large eighteenth-century manor house faces south east over a wide lawn, grandly punctuated by four rows of statues and giant Irish yews, leading the eye to the horizon, where wold meets sky beyond the spacious rides in Bruern woods. By contrast, the Red Brick House faces a smaller lawn, with here and there a malus or a prunus tree, and bounded by reeds and water plants edging the pond. Leading from the house, a long Cypress Walk skirts the western edge of the tangly pond, with its wild island inhabited by ducks and geese and its charmingly decrepit boathouse. Beyond it grow huge old willows, glowing red in winter, and further, over a simple stile, lie the water meadows of the Evenlode. This end of the garden, tucked away from the great yew sentinels of the abbey, is perennially romantic, with a natural waywardness rather than a 'wild disorder of the dress'. The water cascading under an elegant stone bridge by the cottage, the call of sheldrake and moorhen on the pond, and of other marsh birds from the meadows, the ragged drifts of daffodils in spring, and the mysterious Cypress Walk, its inky, velvet columns alternating with diaphanous flowering trees, all conspire to an atmosphere of *La Belle au Bois Dormant*.

The transitions between this spellbound garden and the august dignity of the Irish yew lawn, Michael had designed in a masterly series of variations. He was at his happiest as

Hidcote in Gloucestershire (left)

The façade of Bruern Abbey (right) beyond the giant Irish yews on the front lawn

a painter, rather than in his other political and literary *métiers*. Although he sometimes took advice for the garden, for instance from Lanning Roper, his own painter's eye and intimate love of the surrounding countryside were the dominant inspiration in his creating the subtly changing garden views. A rose garden was hidden behind high beech hedges, from whence one heard the gentle plashing of its fountain. But all else was open, an invitation to contemplative wandering through its various walks of shrubs or tapestry hedges, by its marsh garden, or round by the willows to the mysterious Cypress Walk. As one wandered, there were glancing views through trees to further paths, or to the glistening surface of the pond, and passing glimpses of the great, grey abbey or the coral-coloured cottage, their stillness buried or momentarily revealed through a shifting screen of foliage. Every aspect had an atmosphere of relaxed abundance, yet with no hint of the crammed profusion of a Hidcote. The pleasure of Bruern was rather in its quiet and almost magical spaciousness, where to crowd or hurry would have been unimaginable. It was a garden of, and for, reflections.

For stretches of the time that we lived there we were each immersed in our work, Stephen upstairs writing poetry, Michael over at the abbey painting, or writing *Tribal Feeling*, whilst I was often learning new repertoire for concerts. Especially I recall a season in early summer when, between sessions at the piano, I would enjoy felicitous meanderings through the grassy paths where watery sounds filled the air, my mind entirely possessed by Liszt's visionary *Les Jeux d'Eau à la Villa d'Este* and his stark and monumental 'Cypress' pieces from the third *Année de Pèlerinage*. On one of these evenings, plunged deep in musi-

*Red Brick Cottage, as it was known in our
day, a Queen Anne dower house*

cal thought, I was halfway along the Cypress Walk when I suddenly became aware of
Michael approaching, similarly engrossed in his writing. Too late to turn back – desirable
not to interrupt the flow of his thought – social small-talk unthinkable! As we came near I
murmured what Sir George Sitwell, raising his hat, had said to Arthur Waley when meet-
ing halfway round the lake at Renishaw, each on a solitary early-morning walk – 'What a
pity we are not going in the same direction' – and passed on. Brief chuckles set each of us
free for our creative preoccupations.

For recollection in tranquillity, at Saint-Jérôme we are blessed with the eternal setting
of the crags. Yet the garden itself had to be made so that the interior monologue may
calmly flourish as one strolls the paths. This ideal, with one's backward gaze at Bruern, was
sometimes not easy to reconcile with our *terrain* of very limited proportions, and the ever
hungry passion for crowding in the new plants we continued to discover. Yet we all find it a
place in which we can readily be immersed in work. Stephen could be seen three or four
times in a working day, wandering round looking happily absorbed. At seven one early
morning, as I was dead-heading roses, I seemed to hear the intermittent sound of a wood-
pecker. This was so unusual that, thinking perhaps to astonish my ornithologist friends, I
crept, stalking it as silently as I could, down the Lilac Walk, only to find at the end our
guest, John Bayley, typewriter on knees, humming benignly to himself before tapping out
the next sentence.

Funtington, Monk's House, Sissinghurst, Hidcote and Bruern; here then were the varied
images of verdant grace and plenty which furnished my mind as I began, in 1965, to design

the foreground to our mountain view. They were all mature gardens which had been continuously tended by owners and their gardeners. They were nurtured by the moderate English climate with its days of melting rain that are so kind to plants, and above all they appeared to have flourished for decades in their present felicity. But my reality in Provence was in almost laughable contrast to them: a harsh, hot climate, the ground baked hard in summer, no water to spare for gardening, poor, neglected, excessively limey soil; no gardener; and myself only a sporadic though hard-working visitor. As the house faced due south, the violent mistral roared at our backs, and whipped the powder dry soil from the old vine roots. The site was enveloped in a cloud of cement dust, and at the eastern end of the field, the shell of the scaffolded, half-restored house, and a hideous tin Nissen hut storing the necessities of construction, were surrounded by a sprawling litter of builders' rubble. None of all this, however, could even begin to discourage, as soon as one turned towards the south, the sun, and the sublime landscape of this outcrop of the Alpilles.

We reminded ourselves of the wisdom imparted to us by Harold Nicolson, who had described an almost two year hiatus before he and Vita had decided upon the form their garden should take, its main vistas and its enclosures, the relation of formality to informality and to the surrounding woods and fields. Then we had several visits from neighbours who fell in love with the site, whatever the foreground horrors, and who encouraged such ideas as were beginning to germinate in my mind. And best of all, the wild flowers seemed to be in high spirits that year. We seemed to be forever discovering new treasures that clearly cared not a rap for the poor conditions and, neither toiling nor spinning, nodded their way through a radiant season in glorious array. Impatient as we were for builders to depart, for the natural peace of the valley to be restored, and for our competence in ludicrous practical emergencies to improve, it was a time of happy promise for the future.

The olive grove at Saint-Jérôme with the tamarisk and wild cherry trees in the foreground

Looking eastwards towards the 'Val des Amants' from the ruin behind Saint-Jérôme

CHAPTER 3

First Steps

For painters, poets and builders have very high flights,
but they must be kept down

SARAH, DUCHESS OF MARLBOROUGH, ON BUILDING BLENHEIM PALACE

Although I had very soon drawn the outline plan of the garden on squared paper, and the essence of the conception was never subsequently varied, nevertheless for quite a time it had to remain a dream. Clearly my eagerness to plant had had to be restrained while the confusion and occasional bursts of building proceeded. I was at that time taking a degree course at University College, London, and so could only manage to make flying visits. This made progress somewhat slow, since it is a law of nature in Provence that when the client departs, so then do the builders, to another site where their clients are able to scold or to encourage on a daily basis. However, the delay could profitably be used to think about the design of perspectives, and to restore the health of the soil.

This latter need was urgent. So on one of my early visits I approached Monsieur Guérin, an ample smiling figure who looked cheerfully majestic on his tractor, and who did contract ploughing for the apricot and olive farmers of the district. In the first winter of our discontent with building debris, he had removed the old vine stumps, ploughed, and planted vetch. In the following spring this had been ploughed in as a first step in the restoration of the soil, the process being repeated twice, in the following spring and autumn.

The other first step of some urgency was to provide a windbreak. We had already decided that, when finally the time should come, the builders' rubble was to be bulldozed up the sloping terrain towards the house to provide a terrace, which should be completed by a high protective wall on the north side, continuing the line of the back wall of the house. We realized that a wall is deceptively unsatisfactory as a protection against wind, but our desire for wall plants near the house persuaded us to take the risk. Since the barren terrain behind the house was seven feet higher than our field (its retaining wall long since disintegrated), I asked the farmer who owned it whether we might buy it, or at least a strip bordering our

The house prior to the building of the terrace wall and planting of the cypress windbreak

The house finished with the rectangular enclosed garden ready to be planted

property, since he was not cultivating it. The idea was to plant a row of cypresses on the higher level, thus more rapidly creating a high, effective windbreak. But he not only refused my request, but also pointed out that it was exceedingly accommodating of him not to require us to dismantle our scaffolding and block up our planned north-facing windows which, he said, he had every legal right to do. Inexperienced as we were in some neighbourly tactics which are customary in Provence, we devoted ourselves to an exercise in mollification. Relations between us became more affable, but the refusal remained. A decade later his son and heir sold us the field together with a large olive orchard.

Meanwhile, continuing the line of the terrace wall, we planted our windbreak of knee-high cypresses on the lower level. We put up a *canisse* fence to shelter them in their infancy, and watered them in through the summer using the scant supply from our well, often supplemented by a small tanker-load brought from the village. They all survived. Apart from these few practical measures all my effort went into thinking about the design. It was an effort far from arduous, however, for the main axes seemed self-evident, and barren as it might seem, the terrain was a *tabula rasa*.

Extending laterally east-west from the house the field could only be described as a quadrilateral. It was clear that the windbreak should delineate a vista straight to the west, towards a corner enclosed on two boundaries by much higher ground. This extremity of our land was far from barren since a dense *garrigue* had encroached from the steep and formerly terraced hillside rising to the rocks at the west. Consequently the boundary could only be guessed at by the *géomètre*, a sharp and rather dour fellow who was naturally unwilling to brave his way through this impenetrable thicket of punishing prickles. As in the house where, there being no right angles in the roughly built *bergerie*, the positions of bedroom walls could only be decided by the builder and I standing on bare joists at opposite outside walls and stretching bits of string between us to mark the lines, so, out of doors, any straight walk would have to alternate with one of irregular contour if the garden were to take its shape happily within the wild. We ideally wanted the differing aspects of the view to come as a gentle surprise as one walked. Our further aspiration – if this could be achieved without giving the feeling of a conscious effect – was that the view from the house and from parts of the walk should, in the foreground, echo the lines of nature, rather in the spirit of the Japanese 'borrowed landscape'.

The intention was to extend the idea of borrowed landscape not only to line but also to colour and forms. Standing where the terrace would be, the uninterrupted view of *pinède* and crags seemed to demand that the foreground be planted with a kind of *maquis*, though in all probability one composed largely of cultivated shrubs and flowers. Here colours would melt into each other, and lead the eye to the middle and then further distance. Any more formal treatment of that space would seem glaringly artificial, only marginally less shocking than, say, a French parterre. As the garden extends westwards, however, the view becomes increasingly fragmented into smaller perspectives, so that in this area there would

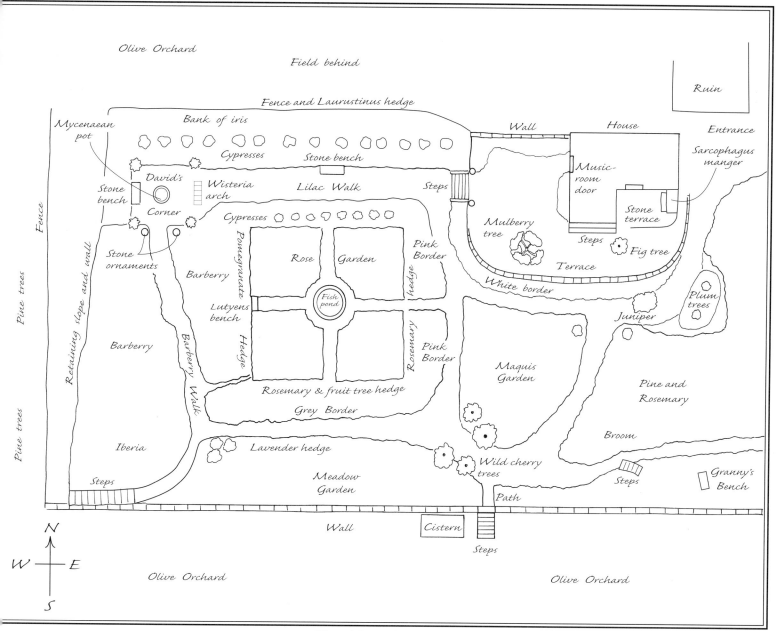

Olive Orchard

Field behind

Ruin

Fence and Laurustinus hedge

Wall   House   Entrance

Bank of iris

Mycenaean pot

Cypresses   Stone bench   Sarcophagus manger

Stone bench

David's   Wisteria   Lilac Walk   Steps   Music-room door

Corner   arch

Stone bench

Cypresses   Stone terrace

Stone ornaments   Mulberry tree   Steps   Fig tree

Retaining slope and wall

Fence

Pine trees   Barberry   Rose   Garden   Pink Border   Terrace

Pomegranate Hedge   White border   Plum trees

Lutyens bench   Fish pond   Juniper

Barberry   Rosemary hedge   Pink Border

Barberry Walk   Maquis Garden   Pine and Rosemary

Pine trees   Rosemary & fruit tree hedge   Broom

Grey Border

Iberia   Lavender hedge   Wild cherry trees   Steps   Granny's Bench

Steps   Meadow Garden   Path

N

W   E   Wall   Cistern   Steps

S   Olive Orchard   Olive Orchard

Plan of the garden as it stands today

*The steps into the garden from the olive grove
and the tamarisk in the Maquis Garden,
echoing the lines of nature*

View of the Grey Walk (opposite) from Iberia

be the freedom to choose plants in a more 'designed' spectrum of colours. And to accommodate our desire for walks, there could be a central enclosed garden, its hedges serving as background to the borders of the walks.

With all these purposes in mind, the main design seemed to solve itself in the simplest fashion. Placing the rectangular enclosed garden to the south-west of the terrace would enable its longer, northern side to form one backdrop to the long walk of our windbreak. With the dark green of the cypresses once they had matured (our thoughts ran on), what better than to use only white and perhaps the palest mauve flowers in borders which would be, by their orientation and height, fresh in spring, and obscured from the beating sun of high summer? Moreover, the natural slope of the terrain was such that we should need a flight of steps down from the terrace to the walk, a descent into subtle, ghostly colours of quiet and cool.

Next, at the far end of this walk, in the boundary angle at that time consisting of horribly daunting *maquis*, we planned to clear a square in which to place the focal monument of the walk (in the event, the 'Mycenaean' pot). We could make of the square a shady retreat with a seat from which to see both this white walk vista toward the house and, starting at right angles, a path winding gently south through a comparatively wild garden outside the

shorter edge of the rectangle. The idea of less formality here was evoked not only by the encroaching hillside pines and undergrowth, but also by the view beyond the end of the envisaged path. This prospect is of an outcrop of rock two fields away, a great thin slab with a single slender pine growing, dramatically oblique, against its flat vertical surface. The view gives unforeseen pleasure since it is not visible until one has turned the corner at the square into this path. I thought of this garden as being bronze and autumnal in tone, dotted with brilliant splashes of scarlet, coral and orange to enliven the atmosphere created by the overhanging pines, perhaps some purple foliage, and then berberis heavy with berries, arbutus, persimmon and flaming pomegranate.

David's corner beyond the wisteria arch spanning the end of the Lilac Walk

Turning the second corner would bring one to the long, straight border outside the southern edge of the rectangle, where there would be the beating Mediterranean sun all day long in summer, and a full view of the range of limestone rocks. Here would be the place for the felted greys, the yellows and the blues which thrive in sites of hot aridity. Of course, the whole garden is under Mediterranean skies, but these colours would be more appropriate to the southern aspect, reflecting the glinting pallor of olive trees below the jagged skyline grey. I had to bear in mind, as well, that this walk would be an approach to the Maquis Garden in front of the house, and that that garden's visibility from the Grey Walk would favour a gentle transition of forms and colours, avoiding sudden, and perhaps jarring contrasts.

The area to be enclosed within the rectangle, envisaged as a place for spending hours of peaceful reading, we wanted to be a scented garden. We somehow had not arrived at imagining it in any greater detail, though Stephen had the temerity to suggest a central fountain. At this epoch of severe water famine it seemed delightfully beyond our wildest dreams, introducing a vision of ancient Persian opulence.

Even the scheme thus far described seemed wild enough, when one considered the building problems, water famine and shortage of resources in those days of exchange controls. And in any case I was resolved upon counting the pennies and accomplishing the project with my one pair of hands. Looking back, there is reason to gasp at the gap of credibility that in my ignorance I imagined could be closed by the work of these hands. Yet

Matthew painting the shutters

The garden planned and well under way with the cypresses and rectangular garden

in all essentials the original plan has survived and fulfilled those early dreams. In the first year's turmoil of building, however, the only possible practical activity was the tender loving care of our infant cypresses – shaggy ones of Provençal rusticity, rather than the slim, elegant Italian species.

That first summer, in 1965, when Stephen and I attempted to camp out in the one end of the house which had a roof – though as yet no doors and only cement floors – I remember as characterized by clouds of dust eddying in the mistral. The *bergerie*, which was to be our future living room and family bedrooms, remained a tree- and rubble-filled hole in the ground surrounded by crumbling walls. But the little house itself promised to be snug. There the rooms were small but exactly suited to our needs; entrance hall, bathroom, dining room and kitchen below, with our bedroom and Stephen's large library above. On a passing neighbourly visit, however, I am afraid that the evolutionary humanist scoffed at this scheme, saying that our family should need only a ground floor entirely living room, and a first floor entirely dormitory, and that we had hopelessly misunderstood the 'way of life'. He threw up his hands and left. We soldiered on, our happy obstinate way.

The well had been cleaned, and was served by a small petrol-engined pump, which made a wheezy phut-phut noise like that of the old motorboat in which, some years previously, we had explored the coastline of Corfu. However, in high summer the water supply turned

49

out to be dangerously meagre, so that this nostalgia-ridden sound was to be heard, at most, only once a day. We learned the habits of frugality when turning on the brand-new brassy taps. There were also daily trips to the village drinking water fountain, where we would fill our huge glass jars, encased in their straw and wooden slats. We cooked by a camping-gas ring. Lighting (indeed, for the next seven years or so, until the arrival of electricity) was by Aladdin lamps, and a small camping generator, which would give us four hours of brighter light before, in midsentence, we were plunged again into darkness. A scramble for the flashlight, a stampede with the petrol can to the back of the house, a crank at the starter, and we were once again restored to civilized illumination.

Our little gas-powered refrigerator taxed our skill, since persuading it to undertake its task resembled the election of a pope. A burning, petrol-soaked taper was pushed through a long groove, whereupon the chimney at the back would belch an acrid black smoke. With eyes smarting and throat aching one would make numerous such attempts, until a single final puff of purest white would herald the machine's consent to accept its high office in our household.

Monsieur Lopez, the builder, had become central to our lives. He was a man of middle height and wiry strength, with twinkling dark brown eyes in a lean face, bronzed and Spanish-looking, and an air of energetic competence. There was something almost heroic about him. He was a master of the traditional skills and style, of the walls of *pierre apparente*, of upper floors supported by huge, rough-hewn log beams, of keystones and chimneys in the *pierre de Fontvieille*, and of the various ways of laying the hand-made tiles of pale terracotta. However, his various enterprises claimed him, and on occasion it was far from easy to track him down. His workmen, with their cheery Provençal charm, were similarly engaging yet at times equally elusive. Rescuing our ruin from its abandoned state could have its dramatic moments, as when, one day, the ring of workmen engaged in hacking down a corner of rubble wall suddenly sprang apart and backwards. Monsieur Lopez

At work in the garden, the cypresses already high along the north side

*Anne Moynihan, Francis Wishart,
Rodrigo Moynihan and myself considering
proportions of windows*

strode in and, rapidly seizing a spade, advanced master-fully, like a latter-day Saint George, and plunged it upon the neck of a 'viper'.

I was the sole architect of the rebuilding, having made all the drawings used by the builders. Thus my role in the last frenzied rush to complete at least the little house, was to make sure that my intentions were fulfilled. It was imperative to be an early riser, for in summer the work-men would arrive at 6.30 am and the chances were that by 6.45 they might already have made a mistake. One such failure of comprehension occurred when I had ordered rectangular paving stones of various sizes and proportions for laying a small terrace in the angle of the L-shaped house. By 6.45, the stonemason, having care-fully sorted them into uniform stacks, was laying a row all of the same size and shape together. After his initial irritation at my objections he became quite fascinated with the game of fitting the different shapes haphaz-ardly, and was pleased with the final effect of a rustic improvisation.

Hitherto my flying visits had found me either lodged as a solitary guest at the little auberge in the village square, or in the comfort – spiritual as well as physical – of the Domaine de Saint-Estève, the home near Lambesc of our friends Anne Dunn and Rodrigo Moynihan. They had married a few years earlier and, both being painters, had an unerring and original eye for its character in restoring the château. Their memories of their building vicissitudes were still green, so Anne's fellow feeling and encouragement were wonderfully restoring at the end of each day of my grappling, battling, and occasionally exulting.

In the race against time to make our little house habit-able for the arrival of my family, the cement floors were at last covered with the beautiful hand-made tiles of the locality, terracotta hexagons in the kitchen and diago-nally laid rectangles in the hall, while the dining room had glowing, glazed *romaines* of cardinal red. Then came the day of the imminent arrival of Stephen, who was

motoring from England with a philosopher friend of ours. As yet, however, we still had no doors at all within the house, none for the rooms, nor even for the loo and bathroom. My influence with the village carpenter was nil; neither smiles, pleas nor threats prevailed. I drove over to Saint-Estève that evening in a state of exasperation and despair. As so often before, Anne surrounded me with comfort and encouragement. 'Sometimes,' she said dreamily, 'I found, here, that the only thing that worked was tears.'

Nothing was further from my vigorously irate thoughts on the following morning, but on visiting Monsieur Lopez's office I surprised myself by suddenly bursting into tears of rage. I certainly surprised Monsieur Lopez. He rose slowly to attention behind his desk, took off his beret, clasped it to his chest, and watched in reverent wonder. Then, without a word, he left the office and marched down the village street, like an Iberian Gary Cooper in *High Noon*. Trailing after him, I arrived in the *atelier* of the carpenter in time to hear it reverberating with the Lopez Pronouncement: '*Pour nous autres, le client est ROI.*' By that same evening our bathroom and bedroom doors were finished and installed. Our guests were assured of their privacy.

Stephen and the philosopher arrived the following afternoon. During the long drive they had discussed, with some intensity, what they valued most in life. The philosopher asserted that one thing was anathema to him. Lowering his voice to express his distaste confidentially, he said that it was '. . . Luxury'. Of all the hazards to be encountered at Saint-Jérôme, cement dust, smoking oil lamps, water famine or mistral – luxury was to prove to be no problem to him at all.

This day made the turning point from dreams and frustrations to the reality of our Provençal habitation. Henceforth, domestic tribulations or no, we should be in happy residence. To celebrate our jubilance, we gave a housewarming picnic in the field, during which I occasionally described how the garden would be. Our guests, including a large party from Saint-Estève, were smilingly indulgent, too polite to show their incredulity. Very soon afterwards, the entire team of builders departed for their summer holiday, and we were at last free to pursue our ideas for the garden.

We made it a time of exploring the natural habitat of the flowers and shrubs which flourish in the Alpilles, and further afield in the limestone uplands of the Cévennes and the Vaucluse. Indeed, my unfamiliarity with the climate and natural flora was clearly the next problem with which we would have to engage. The kindness of an English climate was denied us, and I certainly did not want to resort to the garish Riviera colours of the cultivated plants which so often seemed the only varieties offered in the local nurseries as being suitable to the climate. So I decided to study which species originated in habitats similar to ours, some cultivated varieties of which I could perhaps bring from English nurseries. In those days, not only was the choice in local nurseries unbelievably restricted, but the notion of wild gardens was unknown. Since we hardly knew the country to the north west of us, furthering our garden education gave us many pleasurable excursions.

The wild Euphorbia characias *planted in the Pink Border*

CHAPTER 4

Flora Far and Near

I went fully fifty times to Montmajour to look at this flat landscape [. . .]
with someone who is not a painter, *and when I said to him 'Look,*
to me that is as beautiful and as infinite as the sea,' he said – and he knows the
sea – 'For my part I like this better *than the sea, because it is no less infinite,*
and yet you can feel that it is inhabited.'

VINCENT VAN GOGH, LETTER TO THEO, 1888

In our first year of residence, in 1965, we had missed the spring flowers and fruit tree blossom of the earlier season, which were to be the revelation of the following Easter holidays. We had, of course, lingering memories from previous fleeting April visits. But in July-August that year, as soon as we had moved in, we were in the season of '*les grandes chaleurs*'. In all Mediterranean climates rain falls from October to April, and summers are extremely hot and dry. Consequently the rampant season of wild flowers is over early. By high summer many have shed their seeds and disappeared, though there are still shrubs which flower in the heat – myrtles, Jerusalem sage and phillyrea. Then there are the natives of Greece, the oleanders, which though originally imported, will often survive in the wild without attention, depending on the conditions. They have long been cultivated in our region.

However, in that same year I had had the pleasure of arriving before the end of the season of broom, intoxicating with its honeyed scent. There were large patches of its brilliant yellow in the *maquis* and bordering the roads. *Spartium junceum* seems to seed itself with great abandon, and we gathered great armfuls of it for the house, without leaving the slightest dent in its profusion. Some of the rosemary was still in bloom, though it is usually at its peak earlier in the year. Through the summer there had followed wave upon wave of colour flushing the grey-green surface of the *maquis*. Jerusalem sage (*Phlomis fruticosa*) had quite a long season after the broom had at last waned.

The wild flowers which had given us such pleasure in our first year of discovery – the marigolds and poppies, the flax and the daisies – were over, as were the drifts of the intense blue muscari and the pale mauve patches of wild thyme in bloom. But then, quite suddenly after the yellow broom, there appeared in the olive orchards some tiny wild gladioli of a deep

The Route du Destet leading to Saint-Jérôme;
Cistus x purpureus *in the Maquis Garden*
(below) and Cistus albidus *brought in from*
the hillside (opposite)

magenta hue, and the verbascums. These were not the very tall woolly spires native to Greece, but *Verbascum longifolium* (syn. *undulatum*) with its crinkled, almost scalloped foliage. There were also the wild garlics, and then the delightful little globes of a steely blue echinops, and later still, the sky-blue catananches. All this time, the new growth of the *cannes de Provence*, which resembles a coarse bamboo, was thrusting upwards until in high summer it reached seven feet or more. It is grown commercially for making the *canisse* screens and windbreaks; but it has so naturalized in the landscape as to remain in great thickety clumps wherever encouraged by the sun.

In July and August the lower *maquis* of our view was filmed with white of wild clematis, whilst honeysuckle, looking like *Lonicera etrusca*, ramped over shrubs and pine trees. By the roadsides there were clumps of the smoky red valerian (*Centranthus ruber*) and of the bright, yolk-yellow 'Scolyme d'Espagne'. The decorative foliage whorls of *Euphorbia characias* remained pleasing, their flowers long since dried out, and very soon the wild myrtle was coming into bloom.

The limestone peak which dominates our view, though appearing as monumental as the Alps, we soon discovered takes only twenty minutes or so to reach from our house. One walks down the lane and across a large apricot orchard, after which there is a scramble over rocks and through *garrigue* to the summit. There we found the dwarf shrubs like box and the spiny *Euphorbia acanthothamnos* weathered into shapely mounds. Between them are dotted the variety of small succulents, sedums, saxifrage and saponaria which cling to the shallow crevices, their solitary tufts resisting the mistral, much as sea anemones resist the waves. A little lower down on the slopes we saw innumerable bushes of the felty grey-green *Cistus albidus*, and we looked forward to the papery, shocking pink flowers which would cover the mountainside from early April.

Already, almost on our doorstep, we had found an abundance of wild and colourful vegetation, which suggested that we should have little need to search further for plants which could naturally thrive on the sporadic care offered by an absentee gardener. Nevertheless, we spread our explorations abroad into the surrounding countryside. There was a favourite, longer Alpilles expedition initiated that summer with our friends Terry and Joanna Kilmartin, who lived close by in the valley. It came to be known as the *Promenade Facile* for its resemblance in miniature to one so called by our guides when we had stayed in the Swiss Alps, near Gstaad. Our Alpilles version consisted in driving to the highest peak above Saint-Rémy, called La Caume, where there is a rather bleak radar station commanding breathtaking distant views. Leaving the car there to be picked up later, we would walk along the crest of the ridge until it narrowed into a very constricted rocky ledge. Following this ledge path some way, we would then scramble down a steep, stony scree to the south, and follow a dry streambed which eventually passes by the mysterious Château de Pierredon, with its giant enveloping plane trees and its screaming peacocks. A little further on the path emerges on the Route du Destet, not far from our house.

Iris *'Dancer's Veil' surrounded by the small
white clusters of* Choisya ternata

*The Maquis Garden dominated by the yucca,
seen from a bedroom window*

On the ridge, the crest is windswept even on the calmest day, a favourite haunt of the gliders from the little airfield below, which swoop in towards one like giant condors. Yet in spite of its exposure to flailing winds, there is very little of the bare rock visible, and an abundance of the low growing shrubs clinging defiantly to anchor. In the following spring we found many more treasures on the *Promenade Facile*, including tiny tulips like a kind of diminutive *Tulipa clusiana*, marbled dwarf iris in yellow and brown, and, best of all, a few of the miniature narcissi which also grow in great scented drifts around the Pont du Gard.

Our curiosity led us further afield, and very soon we were exploring the Camargue, which lies just beyond our marketing town of Arles, and from whence, turning towards the north-east, one can see the line of the Alpilles which embraces Saint-Jérôme. Though captivating as landscape, with its huge skies reminiscent of the low countries of Rembrandt and Constable, and its shining expanses of salt-marshes and *étangs*, it was an alien habitat, whose flora could give us little inspiration for planting our hot and limey hillside. Much more in tune with our own *paysage*, though without its dramatic contours and patchwork of orchards, were the endless bleak Causses of the Cévennes behind Nîmes. They are windswept limestone plateaux which lie above those deep gorges in which the wind has eroded stone into gaunt monuments, almost as fantastic as those of Les Baux. Here we found stunted box, coloured at times by an unusually intense coral-orange. The wispy carpet of turf, close cropped by innumerable herds of sheep and goats, was dotted with frail campanula, flax, convolvulus and scabious, and there were large patches of dried out thistles. It was encouraging to find that in conditions rather less kind than our own, nature can accommodate a delicate diversity of plants. Slightly more to the north-east, high above the deep canyon of the Gorges de l'Ardèche, there is a similar though more wooded plateau which abounds in wild Judas trees, rose-pink in springtime, and in the evergreen *Arbutus unedo*. Our own *Arbutus unedo*, planted soon after this expedition, now towers high beyond a corner of the Rose Garden, giving mistral-proof shelter.

It was time to collect our thoughts, and to relate the species we had found in neighbouring terrains to their family relations from other comparable climes. It was by now evident that we could have made an entirely wild garden, though this might have had a longer drab and colourless season in high summer than we should have wished. So, rather than plant our Maquis Garden entirely with indigenous species, it would be more attractive were we to mingle them with varieties from much further afield. I thought of Mexico, some parts of which are high enough to have a similar range of seasonal heat and cold, where I had seen *Choisya ternata* and colletias growing in profusion. A friend told me that our climate was not unlike the Karoo of South Africa. Then I remembered our travels in California, where wild ceanothus thrives even in areas of summer drought, where in the central valley I had seen broad, misty blue tracts of wild lupin (though these would not have flourished in our alkaline conditions), and where sprawling clumps of Indian paintbrush soften the rough edges of country roads. But above all, it was the entire Mediterranean basin which inspired trains of speculative thought, in particular the Iberian peninsula, Greece and the Balkans.

If *Cistus albidus* could flourish so generously on our hillside, why not try *Cistus ladanifer*, which I remembered having seen growing wild in the Algarve? I had been captivated by its white single blooms with chocolate central splashes when staying some years previously at Saltwood Castle in Kent. Or perhaps *Cistus palhinhae*, its near relation, which I had seen in huge masses clothing the bleak exposed headland of Cape Saint Vincent, with its low-growing mounds covered in large white blooms, like a carpet of blanched dog roses? If it could tolerate those punishing Atlantic gales, surely it would take kindly to our mistral? The Montpellier rock rose to be found in Spain and Portugal is reputedly from the Herault region behind Montpellier, about forty miles from our

Osteospermum *'Whirlygig'*

house. Although I had hitherto not found it there, I came upon it in *maquis* on the north side of the Alpilles sometime later. Or indeed, why not *Cistus laurifolius*, with its flowers like large paper-white poppies with golden eyes? Then the nursery hybrids of these sturdy varieties are legion, so we became avid to explore the local nurseries, expecting them to offer us an abundance of variety.

The curious fact was that in the late 1960s I could find none of these cistus native to Southern Europe in the local nurseries, nor even *Teucrium fruticans*, the shrubby germander which comes from those countries and from North Africa. The paucity of choice left me in some astonishment. The only buddleia then on offer was the ordinary mauve *davidii* (no 'Lochinch' available), though occasionally one caught sight of a 'Black Knight'. Not an old-fashioned rose to be had, nothing but varieties of the order of 'Papa Meilland', 'Peace' and 'Super Star'. Above all, the nursery proprietors of those times used repeatedly to tell me that in Provence white flowers were seen as insipid, if not abhorrent, and therefore they would say with a shrug that such shrubs were '*naturellement*' unobtainable. Only one variety of ceanothus was sometimes in their catalogues, but to ask for its further identification as to variety was to provoke incomprehension, and to assert that there exist nigh on threescore varieties elsewhere in the world met with total incredulity. The quality of their preferred

Cistus *x* cyprius *in the Lilac Walk*

stock – for instance of wisteria, bignonia, rosemary – was excellent, but our visits invariably left us discouraged.

Times have changed since then, and some other varieties of cistus are now available, as are some of the old-fashioned roses, and there has been a surge of interest in many herbaceous strains beyond the hitherto ubiquitous cliché plants. At last, after 20 years or so, local nurseries have become interested in varieties long popular in England. This is largely the result of the influence of certain inspired gardeners who more recently settled in Provence, notably Roderick Cameron at Les Quatres Sources in the Vaucluse. To see his tall, elegant figure strolling the large collections of commonplace plants in relaxed conversation with nurserymen was to understand how their horizons gradually became broadened. The Baronne de Waeldner had already made a fine garden in the north of France, and she too, after settling at a house on the slopes of the Mont Ventoux, had an immense influence on the nurseries of her region, so much so that, through ideas gleaned while exhibiting at Chelsea, their proprietors have become increasingly wide-ranging in their choice of plants hitherto unknown in the south. Once discovered, the plants brought from England can spread like an epidemic through the various market stalls of southern Provence. A friend who came to visit us at South Cottage in Sissinghurst one year fell enamoured of *Osteospermum* 'Whirlygig' and took it back to a nurseryman of his acquaintance near Tarascon. Before a couple of seasons had passed it had appeared not only at the flower festival of that town, but as far away as Cavaillon, Carpentras and Montpelier, and its popularity seems unstoppable. Indeed, year by year the great Floralies festival at Tarascon gained in versatility, for there began to be a surge of adventurousness which continues to surprise and delight all the gardeners of the region.

But in the late sixties there was little prospect of finding locally the plants which possessed one's imagination at that time and for that place. Nevertheless, our first attempt to establish the main features of the Lilac Walk happened in the following autumn of 1966, before I could either take a load from England or even go there myself, for my university term claimed me during the planting season. I had managed to design the walk on a large roll of cartridge paper, and Stephen took a holiday break between books and went with Francis Bacon and David Plante to translate my plan into action.

Some of the plants had already been ordered at a local nursery, starting with those destined to front the row of cypresses. Here we chose a regularly spaced succession of white buddleia (to be imported), white oleander and, as we thought, white lilac, to give a high growing vista of bloom at different times in summer. However, when at last they came into flower some of the lilacs were mauve, for Stephen in his horticultural ignorance had been supplied with what the nurseryman happened to have in stock. So by the time it was discovered, and the trees happy enough in our difficult conditions, we decided to make a virtue of the aberration by softly echoing the lilac tones at ground level. They were underplanted with white irises interspersed with some of palest mauve, to which we added the delicate

A beautiful iris in the Grey Walk, bought in the Floralies at Tarascon as 'Jane Phillips'

Opposite: Stephen and David Plante laid the foundation of the Lilac Walk in the autumn of 1966

Iris 'Rosy Veil', which I am now unable to replace and mourn its disappearance from the catalogues. 'Rosy Veil' has the finest tinge of violet edging the white standards and falls, so much more tender and airy than its more flamboyant and insistent cousin, 'Dancer's Veil'. In front of them have been planted at intervals some pale and lacy artemisias. The general effect on the north side of the walk came to be one of light and misty regularity.

The border to the south side of the path is much wider, and is punctuated at the back by different high-growing shrubs bought locally that first autumn. There was a *Magnolia grandiflora* at the terrace end of the walk, then a large *Viburnum rhytidophyllum*, a photinia, and at the far end a *Yucca gloriosa*. Between these tall punctuation points we planned to have a border more episodic in character, to contrast with that on the northern side. The most hardy and least thirsty of the intervening shrubs were a *Choisya ternata* (still going strong after 25 years, and having two flowering seasons in April and October), and a *Cistus laurifolius* which Stephen brought in his suitcase and which grew to eight feet tall in no time at all. Others of the shrubs bought locally fared less well; the callicarpas languished in the drought, as did the deutzia. Only the well-known *Spiraea* 'Bridal Wreath' seemed exuberantly happy, however little it was given to drink.

Stephen's autumn expedition had been felt by all three friends to be not only a horticultural adventure but also a golden interlude of inspiration with which Provence endowed them. Whilst Francis was wandering the sites of Van Gogh's years of painting in Arles and Saint-Rémy, Stephen and David applied themselves to deciphering and fulfilling my plan. When he had first been invited to accompany Stephen 'to plant trees', David had imagined that it was to be some stylish, municipal ceremony where, surrounded by enthusiastic onlookers, Stephen would throw a token spadeful or two of earth on to the base of a tree held by an official. This unlikely dream, out of character for Stephen to say the least, was quickly blown away. The reality was to stand alone in our scruffy field, buffeted by a biting wind in which the cartridge paper flapped uncontrollably, trying to match up the plan to the state of our unkempt terrain as it then was.

As David tells me, Monsieur M., a Provençal nursery man, delivered the plants and saw at once that help and directives were needed. He was wearing a sagging blue overall with a black belt cinched tightly at the waist, and thick black shoes. He listened to Stephen as if torn between following his instructions and telling him what they ought to be. He took the plan, turned it to the right orientation, indicated where the holes should be dug, and left. On a subsequent raw and frosty late-November day, the pouches of earth containing what seemed puny twigs of shrubs were arranged in their allotted positions. But David was astonished to find that, far from this being an effortless ceremony, the earth was so solid as to be amenable only to attack by pickaxe. On that morning only three holes, not nearly wide or deep enough, had been dug and their plants stomped in, when Monsieur M. reappeared, looking anxious. He obviously wanted to tell them that they weren't doing the work as it should be done, but was too respectful forthrightly to give voice to such a critical notion. He did manage to explain that the ground was too frozen, and that they must not derange themselves, but that he could wait for better weather and finish the job for them.

Stephen and David went off, shivering, to meet Francis in an old Saint-Rémy restaurant with an interior of dark wood panelling, where a carafe of wine and a steaming soup tureen with an old dented ladle were put on the table. They felt thankful for the atmosphere of good, peasant fare, warmth and hugger-mugger, and had a sense of celebrating their accomplishment – or was it their deliverance? Afterwards, culture superseded horticulture, and they all visited Montmajour, the Romanesque abbey of noble proportions, with its view across the flat ricefields towards Arles. They marvelled at the hardy stoicism of Van Gogh, who on just such a day of arctic mistral would sit for hours upon the abbey's rocky promontory, painting that same view.

Francis had painted four *Studies for a Portrait of Van Gogh* some eight years previously, a kind of homage based on Van Gogh's wintry picture *Painter on the Road to Tarascon* (1888), which he knew from reproduction as the original was destroyed in the Second World War. These 'Studies' had been painted in a rather hurried yet obsessed state, to complete an imminent exhibition, but his consciousness of Van Gogh's vision was perennial, and he had an intimate knowledge of the letters Van Gogh wrote during his time in Arles, with their descriptions of the privations of his life and of what the Provençal scene in brilliant light demands of the painter. The image of Van Gogh's wintry trampings through this region, particularly on the Route du Tarascon which passes near Montmajour, was very much in Francis's mind as they climbed the steps to the abbey. The plane trees bordering the road have a stark and knobbled look in winter, their forms contorted against the brilliant azure skies, and even more so in the light of the huge orb of a setting sun. Although Francis had once said that he preferred early Van Gogh, this late picture of the artist trudging – almost leaning against the wind – has the atmosphere of toil akin to that of *The Potato Eaters*. The theme is in stark contrast to the euphoria of the fruit orchards in springtime blossom, while both themes share the astonishing development in Van Gogh's treatment of paint which attended his migration to the South, and which possessed the mind of Francis on that day.

Then, as one stands on the high jutting edge of Montmajour, the texture of frozen furrows of bare earth as one looks across the ricefields towards the familiar skyline of Arles is equally evocative of what Francis most admired in Van Gogh, this vitality of texture, achieved by brushstrokes, which intensifies one's vision of reality. Francis himself always strove for this 'complete interlocking of image and paint'. While regretting my absence from that day's expedition, Stephen's description of it made a great impression on the immediacy with which I view the landscape. By looking with the eyes of those two painters, each with his intense feeling for light and the dancing movements in nature, whether of cypresses, spring foliage or human forms, one is nearer to grasping the essential reality of the scene.

Van Gogh's Painter on the Road to Tarascon

Francis Bacon at the abbey of Montmajour in the company of Stephen

When I arrived some months later at Saint-Jérôme I found that, miraculously, Stephen's plants had all survived. The winter conditions in Provence are, to put it mildly, unpredictable, some years warm and frost-free, others more punishing. But that year the fates had been kind. Such is the chancy nature of season for the absentee gardener that it is only having arrived earlier than usual one year, a quarter of a century later, that I first saw the photinia, one of those first puny shrubs to be planted and now towering above us, in full and frothy bloom.

We have often wondered whether the wild flowers should have been given an even warmer welcome in our garden, and it is a perennial game to visualize their taking a greater share. The odd thing is that some of them decline the invitation, while revelling in the aridity of the olive grove below, or the unyielding crevices of the rocks above. Or, when least expected, they will crowd in for a season and just as unaccountably disappear in the following year. I remember a glorious invasion by a host of sedum, which particularly chose any spot where the periwinkles are happy. In due season they grew very long flowering stalks of pale green with fluffy heads and we found them a delightful addition when the flowering vinca was over and had reverted to its glossy green foliage. But the following year there was no sign of them, though they continue to enjoy life in the ruin behind the house, where periwinkles seem very unhappy in the drought of high summer. No doubt they did not care even for the sparse summer watering which seems to encourage them. The small echinops and the wild gladioli were equally reluctant when we tried to coax them the few steps from the olive orchard into the garden. However, it is fortunate that they live and proliferate so happily under the olive trees, and give us such pleasure a stone's throw beyond the garden steps.

A neighbour in those earlier years, whose repeated *sondages* for water had been totally unproductive, was compelled to buy it by the tanker-load for the household. Unable to spare any for the garden he made a simple attractive patch of rosemary, lavender, and santolina in front of the house, and as he was even more absentee than us, it was pleasing to see how it flourished. But before long the water famine finally defeated him, and I believe that, after his departure, his successors decided that a fruit orchard was the best solution. It certainly restored the farming character of the valley, the modern house now scarcely visible beyond the trees.

After contemplating many garden schemes for a simple Provençal *mas*, clearly where there is no water at all, the traditional unpretentious style is best, and can be very harmonious. Fig trees and mulberries, wisteria and honeysuckle all thrive in this climate, and the native broom, phlomis and myrtle give later bloom without tears. But if one is more fortunately able to nurse less indigenous plants through the torrid season, then it would seem that the guiding principle should be to choose plants which originate in similar climates. This was our early resolve, and through the years there has seemed to be no end to the possible variation, certainly more than could be accommodated in an acre of garden.

Prunus *'Okumiyako' (syn.* P. serrulata *'Longipes') in full bloom in the Grey Walk*

CHAPTER 5

Provençal Spring

There is an inexhaustible sweetness
that rests in the grey green landscape of Provence …
It blooms with heath and scented shrubs and stunted olive, and the white rock
shining through the scattered herbage
has a brightness which answers to the brightness of the sky

HENRY JAMES, 'A LITTLE TOUR OF FRANCE', 1885

It was early in the following Easter holidays, in 1967, that I was able to cram the car with my first sizeable load of plants from England and set forth. By that time the apricot and peach orchards south of Lyon were flushed rose-pink in bud, and further south in blossom, though in our own district they would be already on the wane or even over, for there can be quite two weeks precocity in Provence. However, the moment one has passed the huge industrial zone of Lyon and ascended the hill beyond Vienne, the vegetation, and above all the light, have changed from the cold colours bathing the countryside of Burgundian vineyards and the wide valley of the Saône, so often at that season in full flood, with bleak denuded treetops showing above the broad expanses of water. Although the prospect on either side of the road beyond Lyon is bounded by snow-clad peaks of Alps and Massif Central, the light begins to glow with southern warmth and one's spirits begin to rise. Even the snowy summit of Mont Ventoux, some hundred miles or more to the south of Lyon, glows faintly pink behind Orange, and by the time one leaves the fast road at Noves total euphoria overtakes one at the honey-coloured light reflected from the buildings in that little town.

By Easter of that year the *bergerie* at Saint-Jérôme had been reconstructed, and we now had bedrooms enough to accommodate eight people in fairly Spartan style. I had designed a large chimney for log fires, though as yet the sitting room had no furniture other than a large farmhouse refectory table. We managed with garden chairs, until our one permitted load of furniture could arrive from London, for exchange controls precluded our buying locally. However, this rudimentary lifestyle proved no hardship at all, since even at Easter the weather was so radiant that all day could be spent outdoors.

My first consignment of plants, unpacked from the car on arrival, had been ordered from

The prunus during early days of planting the Grey Walk

Opposite: The east terrace (top) shaded by the profusion of Wisteria sinensis *'Plena', and the climbing 'La Follette' (below and detail), a rose indigenous to Provence*

the old Sunningdale Nurseries, which seemed to offer every rose known to man, and whose staff seemed to receive one's visit and to greet whatever problem one presented with enthusiasm and originality. I see from a copy of that order that even then my rosarian desires were pretty disparate, two *Rosa filipes* 'Kiftsgate'; 'Schneezwerg'; 'Frühlingsmorgen'; 'Frühlingsgold'; 'Reine des Violettes' and a 'Francis E. Lester', the latter being the only casualty after a year or two. I remember that the *filipes* had also been inspired by my having seen it climbing to great heights upon the walls of the castle at Saltwood, where a garden is contained within the extensive keep. Seen from below, the hundreds of single blooms in every cluster on high were spectacular, and when walking along the narrow ledge at the top of the battlements the scent was almost overpowering.

At Sunningdale I was also given two wonderfully appropriate suggestions for climbing roses which I had not encountered in England. 'La Follette', which is descended from *Rosa gigantea*, is not hardy so far north, but is to be seen on the Côte d'Azur. For us in Provence it blooms extravagantly in early April (indeed, in the spring of 1988 it started in February), and for the rest of the season its elegant foliage, faintly tipped by a coppery red, now provides a backdrop for the thrusting wands of lemon verbena, an abutilon, a caryopteris and a crimson floribunda rose which we later planted at the foot of the terrace wall, all of which have their season later in the summer. Their other suggestion, a climbing China rose called 'Hermosa', was equally successful. We also chose a *Ceanothus* x *veitchianus* which soon grew large and amazingly floriferous until some eight years later it was blown clean over in a violent mistral.

My first Easter in residence was in fact an old-fashioned 'reading party'. Stephen was away on an American tour, so I invited seven of my fellow students from University College. They were all around 20 years younger than I, but we were so relaxed in style and mutual in our studious concerns, that never for a moment did they let me feel the generation gap. The only firmly organized feature of the holiday was that every evening after dinner we held a seminar on some specific topic from the course. But there was a minimum of forward planning. Someone would volunteer to lead the seminar, as for instance, 'I think on Thursday I'll lead a seminar on Ethological Concepts', just as, in an equally impromptu tone, one of the girls might say at breakfast, 'I think, tomorrow for dinner, I'll cook my very special moussaka.' The boys used to trim and fill the Aladdin lamps and stoves, and drag in firewood from the hillside. Best of all, they would dig the holes for planting my shrubs. The girls loved to do the marketing in Arles or Saint-Rémy, and everyone was eager to take a turn in riding the Mobylette down to the village to fetch fresh croissants for breakfast. The spin for three miles down the hill, through the air of morning already warm and scented with whiffs of rosemary and thyme, was considered the most delectable of treats.

We each read quite hard, for exams were looming. The young would be sprawled on deck chairs or sunbathing on chaises-longues, whilst I was intermittently pottering and

planting in the so-called 'garden'. On the sunny terrace-to-be, textbooks passed from hand to hand in preparation for forthcoming discussion, just as ideas were tossed about in speculative freedom, only to be hammered and hotly disputed in the evening session, in faint Aladdin illumination before a huge log fire. I cannot imagine why, after a day of fresh air, marathon walks or sunbathing, and after a sumptuous evening meal, we did not fall asleep in the firelight. But it was, in truth, the most animated part of the day. On occasion, the clash of intellectual cut and thrust would last until well after midnight before dissolving into jocularity.

Apart from the roses and wall plants, most of the planting that Easter was of indigenous seedling shrubs from the crowded hillside, such as *Cistus albidus* and rosemary. We had enclosed the central rectangle of the garden with a *canisse* fence, though it was to be many years before we were able to cultivate it. But against the fence we hoped to plant the outside hedges with which to back the exterior borders. At the western end, in what was to become the Barberry garden, I made, against the *canisse* fence, an informal hedge of pomegranate which already, later that season, began to flourish its scarlet trumpets. Again as punctuation points, during Stephen's visit there had been placed before it an arbutus, a *Prunus pissardii* and a purple-leaved maple. Somewhat later the remaining two sides of the *canisse* enclosure were planted with apples, pears and quince, trained in candelabra form to make a screen at the back of the borders-to-be. Though all else remained wild at that time, the essential shape was pleasantly delineated.

It was on this spring visit that the larger terrace surrounding the house was built up from the remaining debris. Although the temperature plummeted at sunset, one member of the reading party, a hardy Canadian called Bill MacAlister, preferred to spend his nights in a sleeping bag on a long, plaited-plastic garden chair which was placed in front of the north garden wall, with a large, yellow garden umbrella over him in case of rain. Early one morning all those of us inside the house were awoken by the noisy arrival of the bulldozer. We gathered outside to watch its gargantuan operation, whilst in spite of the grinding clatter Bill slept serenely on, under his colourful umbrella. Nearer and nearer clanked the giant machine, scooping up the tons of builders' rubble towards the wall. Meanwhile the workmen had lit a bonfire, against my protests that after mid-March this is strictly illegal. Within minutes a fire-monitoring helicopter was hovering low overhead, adding to the almost intolerable din. By now the helicopter pilot and the laughing circle of students and workmen watched amazed at Bill's imperturbability until, at the ultimate moment of danger of his summary interment, he opened one eye, stretched and slowly rolled over, and like the beggar of Bethesda, 'picked up his bed and walked'.

The *pierre apparente* retaining wall of this new terrace was quickly built, and with it, the flight of shallow steps in hard, ochre-coloured *pierre de Rognes* (from a quarry near Lambesc) which led down from the terrace to the White Walk. The small paved terrace in the angle of the house had needed a boundary at the driveway end, and so we had placed

The Barberry Walk (right) seen from Iberia with the 'Graham Thomas' rose to the left

A first sight of the cypress and the Rosa filipes
'Kiftsgate' in bloom from the first planting

the sarcophagus-manger from the *bergerie* on a low wall at right angles to the end bollard of the house. We made of it a sink garden with dianthus, dwarf iris, and portulaca and other succulents, and below it on the paving we put a stone seat. This corner became the out-of-doors breakfast room, where one could sit leaning back against the sarcophagus, enjoying the clove-scented air emanating from the cottage pinks.

The rubble of the larger terrace had been compacted and smoothed level by the bulldozer, so we were at once able to cover it with a gravel of small, smooth pebbles. Now I was seized by an overriding ambition to make at least one gravel path in the garden, that in the Lilac Walk. However, there the fight against couch grass proved a more intractable problem than I had foreseen, and we lacked the appropriate tools for making a path, in particular a garden roller. When at last a small start had been made, and for a very few metres at the far end of the walk the ground had been thoroughly cleansed, the problem arose as to how we were to compact and level the surface. 'There's no other way,' said a young member of the party, 'we shall have to jump on it.' So eight of us linked arms and embarked on a vigorously rhythmic, callisthenic routine. The ludicrous sight of this vehement, stomping dance was witnessed by an unexpected caller, the evolutionary humanist. For a moment he gazed sourly at the sight, then turned and fled without even saying 'Good afternoon'.

By the end of the holiday there was a pleasing stretch of path at the end of the walk, gleaming in smooth-stoned gravel. It gave me a disproportionate surge of pleasure and hope, for the shape of the garden was beginning to come into focus. It was no longer a figment in the mind's eye. A fragment of it was formed, like the partial picture which emerges at one corner as one starts a jigsaw puzzle. As we packed all our textbooks and were preparing to leave, my student friends appeared, bearing four small pine trees, one for each corner of the square at the end of the new path. They now form a high, shady canopy above the Mycenaean pot, and on restful afternoons spent reading in this quiet corner, my thoughts often return to the charm of those garrulous, pioneer days, and the generous friendship of my young colleagues.

When Stephen and I returned in late June, we invited the building team to a party to celebrate their achievement, together with some of our English neighbours whose French was more fluent than ours. The terrace looked festive with pink geraniums, the horrid Nissen hut had at last been removed, and the newly pruned fig tree over the well cast a dappled shade. It was an exuberant gathering. Wine was flowing, and the workmen and their wives made quips in Provençal, which delighted them the more when all the Anglo-Saxons looked pleasantly mystified. Monsieur Lopez ceremoniously planted some slips of Virginia creeper next to a bollard as we all raised our glasses to him, and to the branch of flowering broom high overhead which, by Provençal tradition, is attached to the roof of a new house as soon as it is finished.

The Virginia creeper did almost too well. It raced up to the eaves and had to be restrained from grappling the roof tiles loose. Eventually, to cover the metal frame of the

The Wisteria sinensis *'Plena' above the east terrace*

Stephen beneath the bignonia, its bright orange trumpets in full bloom

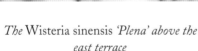

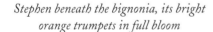

awning, which at first shaded the terrace by *canisse* laid flat upon it, I also planted a bignonia, soon bright with orange trumpets, and a wisteria which proved slow to ascend and inordinately shy of flowering. We discovered some years later that this was because the greedy roots of the Virginia creeper had monopolized all the amenities the ground had to offer, including the drains. When a crisis occurred, the plumber drew from the drain an immensely long, snake-like form, for the roots had extended for very many metres through the pipe into the garden. So, for the sake of hygiene the creeper had to be banished, though even now a tiny protesting shoot will emerge, no doubt still hoping to be welcomed back from exile.

But the moment that the creeper had been sent packing the wisteria started enthusiastically to bloom in early spring, before the leaves appeared. Only then did we realize that this was not the usual *Wisteria sinensis* which we all love, but one in which each flower in the long raceme is a rosette, rather than the familiar pea flower. Since the local nursery seemed quite unconcerned to distinguish the variety, I assume that it must be *Wisteria sinensis* 'Plena'. We had been tempted to have a *Wisteria floribunda* 'Multijuga', but envisaged fighting our way through the long racemes to reach the modestly proportioned front

Pots of geraniums set against the east terrace wall

The view from the terrace shaded by the plane-leaved mulberry

door and so rejected the idea. The bignonia also had a shot at raising the roof, before we persuaded it to luxuriate in shading the terrace, where it blooms in high summer.

The curved retaining wall of the terrace was planted with a lavender hedge which for ten years was a favourite haunt of bees and butterflies. But as it grew ever thicker and taller it took over too much space needed for walking round the well. So it was eventually replaced by a ribbon of low carpeting plants to creep over and soften the edge of the wall, sedums, rock roses, zauschneria, the small *Teucrium* x *lucidrys*, and the sun-loving saponaria.

During those first seasons which succeeded the reading party our water problem remained acute; it governed our choices and somewhat curbed our activities. But choosing a shade tree for the western end of the terrace was simple. The plane-leaved mulberry is very popular in our region since it tolerates drought, and its large leaves provide a comfortable shade. With us it also had to tolerate growing on a diet of the rubble of which the terrace was made, as well as the whip of the mistral over the back terrace wall. Indeed, in its first winter it suffered a violent tearing of branches on the windward side, but as it gained in strength, the torn gap in its canopy was quickly filled. By now it is thriving, and plays host to a *Rosa filipes* 'Kiftsgate' which romps up into its branches. For our meals

The terrace from the garden

outdoors in summer, the mulberry and the rose form a shady, scented enclave where we sit enjoying our view of the rocky limestone ridge as it changes in tone and brilliance with the passage of the sun.

At some time during those years in the late 1960s, we had acquired a stretch of the *pinède* on the hillside, the olive orchard below the garden, and a large olive and apricot orchard which flanks the Route du Destet behind the house. Little was I prepared for the many hours of work which they would need, but it proved to be enjoyable exercise at the seasons both of pruning and of harvest. We had also planted cherry trees, so that the summer has come to be a time not only of delighting us with fresh fruit, but also of days filled with

*Flanking the Route du Destet,
the stretch of land behind the house which we
were finally able to buy*

making jams and jellies, chutneys and *aigres-doux* for delectation in the colder months. This succession of tasks was new to me, and I found my year taking on a new character. The natural cycle of weather and its appropriate duties impart a rhythm which had not previously come my way. In city life one tends to overcome or to compensate for the contrasts of the seasons, congenial though they may be, whereas in Provence they draw one into a harmonious and gentle changing of pace and pursuit as the months go by. There was much to learn, and the manner of its learning so unlike that of music or of scholarship, that I felt ushered into a new existence – almost into living in a different epoch of our civilization.

The wild cherries in bloom above the olive orchard

Apricots and Olives

Earth herself, by the crooked plough laid bare, provides
Moisture enough for the plants and a heavy crop from the ploughshare.
Thus shall you breed the rich olive, beloved of Peace.

Virgil, 'Georgics', Book 2, l.423–425, trans. C. Day Lewis

The Alpilles are surrounded by apricot orchards; the trees bloom in March or early April, some time after the almonds, and are followed by the cherry blossom. Within scarcely three months the fruit is ripened and ready to be harvested. Our weather gives us an earlier crop than occurs further up the Rhône valley, which makes the enterprise even more worthwhile to farmers. Another profitable characteristic is the short time it takes before a newly planted tree bears fruit; the trees have a relatively short life but a highly productive one. Near a neighbouring farm called Monblanc there has been a big replanting in the last three or four years, and already from the foot-high truncated sticks of planting time, the trees have grown tall and bushy-headed, the rich dark green foliage tipped with a bronzy red. Some of them are already bearing fruit.

The small orchard that we had acquired had been well tended. It stands behind the house and commands a wide view of the surrounding peaks which stretches to the imposing Mont-les-Opies behind Eyguières. As with most fruit trees here except for the espaliered apples, the trees are pruned open at the centre, in an inside-out umbrella shape to give them the best of the sunshine. To begin with, the ebullient old Monsieur Blanc used to prune our trees. One day in early July of my first season he screeched his Mobylette to a halt beside me in the village street and, in railing tones, said, 'Why haven't you picked your apricots?' As they were a pallid cream colour and, it seemed to me, bullet firm to the touch, I had been waiting until they would acquire a warm aroma and a glowing orange-coloured pliancy. So I replied in some confusion 'But are they ready?' 'Ready?' he laughingly scoffed, 'they're already *confiture*.'

His timescale, however, was that of the *expéditeurs* who send the fruit on long journeys to distant markets. In the farms the fruit is picked in the very early morning, from soon after five, when it has been cooled by the night air. It is then sorted, the perfect for dessert, the less than perfect for the manufacture of jam. The pickers are mostly ladies from the village who, as soon as the sun begins to warm the trees, retire to the large barns. There, standing at trestle tables, their fingers seem to fly across the mountainous piles of fruit while they chatter and tease, or exchange the latest village news, commenting like domestic Cassandras. Then, soon after nine o'clock, the large lorries of the *expéditeurs* and the manufacturers arrive, are loaded and away again in no time. The less than perfect apricots could well be jam by the evening.

We have few trees, so we have found or invented a large repertoire of uses for apricots. We eat them fresh for breakfast or lunch, and we load all our visiting friends with baskets full. We have created diverse puddings, sorbets and cold soufflés, and when all the jam, chutney, bottled apricot sauce and butter had been made, we used to give all the apricots that remained to the Maison de Retraite, the old-people's home in the village. There two sweetly cheerful nuns, Soeur Régisse and Soeur Rose, received the laden baskets, and we would chat about how to make the dishes and preserves which the old people prefer. It was an annual encounter which I always enjoyed.

Most enjoyable too, are the hours between five and eight each morning in the cool quiet of the orchard, with the fresh smell of the leaves, and often the company of our three cats, Daisy, Tulip and Poppy, who follow me there like Mary's lamb. There are times of day, in particular the very early morning, when the earth seems to have arrested its motion, which one imagines to be like that of a spinning top, and to hang for a moment more like a pendulum at its turn, before gathering the full-tilt momentum of the morning. Each day seems to have this moment of hanging in the balance, just as the year does at the autumn solstice, when there are a few days of breathtaking stillness. One's mood seems to harmonize with the timelessness; one has a reprieve from the 'long littleness of life', from the worries, memories, anticipation and fret. Instead, there is the measured rhythm of picking, as one's eyes seek out the clusters of fruit like light amber globes among the dark foliage, with the pale opaline sky beyond very gradually assuming the warmer tone of the fire opal. The only sounds are the flights and occasional warblings of birds, and the creaking of baskets as one moves them from tree to tree.

But the apricot harvest is the high-summer culmination of a long crescendo in the seasonal tasks, beginning for me in late March with two months or so of pruning olives. This is followed in late May by the cherry harvest and its days in the kitchen of making preserves, and the *aigres-doux* which are such a popular component of hors d'oeuvres. White-heart cherries are not popular in France, though we planted some in those early days, together with many more of the black-fruited *bigarreaux* or *burlats*, the different varieties affording better pollination. Cherries mature earlier than apricots, and we pick them in a more leisured, even haphazard, manner. The trees present no great problem of pruning, nor do the wild cherries and plums which we found growing round the ruin, or which have seeded

Apricots bottled as jam, chutney and sauce

Daisy sitting at the entrance to the Pink Walk, awaiting the morning expedition

themselves since we arrived. The fruit of the wild cherry is a small, tangy *griotte* of an intense sealing-wax red, which makes the most delicious jelly. It sparkles on the trees which chose to take root on the far side of our Maquis Garden, and in springtime the white blossom is an ethereal companion to the rose-pink tamarisk. The plum trees which we found there when we first arrived bear small *mirabelles*, giving a fresh, slightly sharp jelly which is a family favourite. We can be relatively light-hearted about these small crops, cherries coming before, and *mirabelles* after, the abundant and more serious apricot harvest.

More serious still is the cultivation of our olives, as indeed it is throughout the narrow regions of the Midi, close to the Mediterranean coast, where olives have without interruption flourished for centuries. Our two orchards have between them three hundred trees of different varieties, and my initiation into the traditional skills of their care came as a surprise. Even now I feel it is unlikely that I could ever attain that certainty of hand and eye, that seemingly instinctive feel for the health and beauty of the tree, which the locals have learned from their fathers over many generations.

The seasons of the olive year, more than those of any other husbandry, give the region its character. As soon as the advent of spring suggests that the remote chance of frost is ended, over many weeks from March to May people can be seen in the olive orchards around the Alpilles quietly snipping with secateurs and cutting with the little new-moon-

83

shaped pruning saws. It is an unhurried occupation at a time of enjoying the first delicate wild flowers and aromatic scents of spring. The trees are at first bushy with a year's growth of *gourmands* which are seen as greedily gobbling the strength of the tree. They are pruned away leaving elegant, overhanging branches which will bloom with minuscule grape-like clusters of a downy grey. Then, before *les grands chaleurs*, comes the ploughing to render the arid soil receptive to any drop of moisture that nature may provide. Some farmers spray insecticide and spread *engrais*, though we have never done so. In high summer there is also the pruning-away of suckers growing from the base of the tree, then, late in August, if irrigation has been sufficient and olives are plump enough, they are gathered for preserves and *olives cassées*. As our land lies too far from the supply of agricultural water to swell the olives sufficiently for *confiserie*, we gather our entire crop for oil, and our family and friends in London, who like to consume the greater part of it, enquire anxiously about the season's prospects when we return to England. The main crop for oil, the size of which can vary greatly from year to year, is harvested from early November, sometimes lasting into the New Year.

In the Provençal attitude to the cultivation of the olive there is a strong feeling for its past history, which even today carries with it a faint consciousness of sanctity. Our neighbours have inherited olive fields which have been in their families for many generations. Some may be less aware of the long, emblematic history of the olive as symbol of peace and of longevity, yet they often show a rather mystical devotion to it, in spite of the increased effort entailed by recent changes in its profitability, for as they all now agree, it is no longer *rentable*. So, though it is increasingly expensive for them to continue, with labour costs for pruning, ploughing and harvesting forever rising, families work very hard to care for the trees themselves rather than to give up. When people reach the age to relinquish their jobs, they spend their retirement years working at what they can no longer pay others to do. But although whole families give up free days at harvest time, young people working through the week in offices are becoming loath to spend their weekends in the olive groves. The skills which have long been passed down from father to son could peter out, since the middle-aged and elderly may become the last generation to devote themselves to the traditions of their forefathers.

This feeling of a sacred significance to the olive could well have been carried by the oral tradition, even from around 600 BC, when the Phoecians, who came from Greece to colonize Marseille, brought with them their cultivated olive trees and their skills to a land which had previously been primal forest. The hinterland of Marseille surrounding the Étang de Berre as far as Arles and the Vallée des Baux has without interruption cultivated olives for 26 centuries, and the oil of the Vallée des Baux is considered the best in France, even in Europe.

We know that the Greeks had practised pruning and grafting in earlier millennia, for in Homeric times Odysseus sheltered under two shoots of olive growing from a single stock,

The wild cherry, in bloom, and sealing-wax red as it ripens in the early months of summer

the one a natural sucker, while the other had been grafted. From Homeric times comes also the use of olive wood for carving and furniture, for again one is reminded of Odysseus and Penelope, whose marriage bed was carved of olive. In Provence the wood was used through the ages, and one can see museum pieces such as the carved crèche figures of the monastery of Saint-Michel-du-Frigolet. Now in the markets one may buy olive-wood salad bowls and cheeseboards, many of them still carved by hand. The wood has a smooth almost unctuous surface, its grain marked by serpentine streaks in gently contrasting colours of straw, ash, and dusty cinnamon.

The Romans cultivated olives not only for food and cooking oil, but also for the oil used for lighting, to which the innumerable terracotta lamps found at archaeological sites bear witness, as well as for massage at gymnasia and thermal baths. Small wonder that they greatly extended its cultivation throughout the Empire, and in Provence this meant its spreading out from the hinterland of Marseille as far as the Côte d'Azur and the Vaucluse. Traces of olive mills in use before the first century AD have been found at Glanum, the Roman city a few miles from our house in the Alpilles, and at Saint-Blaise in the Crau, as well as further afield at Entremont and Le Brusc. A little later production was greatly augmented at various sites around the Étang de Berre and the important Roman crossroads of Ernaginum, near Arles.

We know from Virgil's *Georgics* that to strike slips of olive wood was the Romans' favoured method of producing trees: 'Nay, marvellous to tell, lopped of its limbs, a mere stick of olive still thrusts its roots out from the sapless wood.' One can assume that this method was imported into Provincia, and certainly our landscape abounds in 'Meagre marl and gravel hillsides' which, Virgil wrote, 'delights in olive trees'. Methods of propagation have scarcely changed since his time, and all agree that, particularly in arid terrains, the well-pruned olive tree is capable of withstanding fierce winds, scorching heat and summer droughts, and yet of giving a rich harvest.

The law of the Roman emperors up to the fifth century AD encouraged the production of olives throughout the Mediterranean empire. Ten years after planting trees, or five years after grafting wild ones, a third of the oil produced had to be paid in taxes. During the Middle Ages this obligation passed to the profit of the feudal seigneur, to whose mill all olives had to be brought, and who thus was paid handsomely in kind for the service of producing the oil. By this time Provençal oil was exported far and wide, even to England where it was used for the treatment of wool in the thriving industry of East Anglia.

Production and export reached a zenith in the eighteenth century, when olive oil was used in making fine toilet soap; indeed, today the stalls in Provence street markets offer soap, made to the traditional recipes, which is much sought after. However, in the year of the Revolution, 1789, there was a catastrophic frost which destroyed most of the olive plantations north of the Alpilles from Aix-en-Provence to Tarascon, after which many of these inland regions changed to vineyards. Only those areas of France with suitable micro-

Vincent van Gogh, The Olive Pickers, Saint-Rémy, *1889*

climates, the Alpilles, Salon, and the shores of the Étang de Berre, remained faithful to the olive. These three areas maintained an unbroken cultivation where others fluctuated, taking to viticulture until, in the late nineteenth century, vines were attacked by the phylloxera disease, then returning to olives until they were again frosted. At the present time the fluctuation is arrested, and large expanses of the Rhône valley are given over to the increasingly successful vineyards and fruit orchards.

During the Second World War, when it was no longer possible to import from North Africa, our local olive industry came into its own and flourished until another catastrophic frost in 1956 necessitated cutting the great old trees to ground level. The roots were then either grafted or encouraged to make three, five, or sometimes even seven shoots which developed into slim trunks in a circle on each ancient root. There followed a few years' hiatus while the trees recovered enough once more to produce full harvests. Thus, in contrast to the monumental old olives to be seen in relatively frost-free Corfu, for instance, in Provence trees are now kept to a height of no more than four metres at the very most, and the fruit is easily gathered from the top with the aid of the *chevalet* – a traditional A-shaped wooden ladder with a third tripod leg, well known from Van Gogh's paintings of the olive orchards around Saint-Rémy. The trees are pruned hard on the inside of the circle of trunks surrounding the old roots. Although one can squeeze in between these slender trunks to harvest from inside the tree, this form of pruning with the centre open to the sky ensures that the greater part of the crop above the height that can be reached from the ground is easily accessible from the *chevalet* outside the circle.

In our first years we were helped at harvest time by the Deffaut family. They had come into our lives in our waterless years. Madame Deffaut had become our crucially essential laundress, and we would deliver large bundles of sheets to their farmhouse on the fringe of the village. We would then sometimes sit in the shade of their huge fig tree, gossiping while helping them to peel fruit or vegetables for the large vat of preserves or *coulis de tomates* which stood simmering on a brazier in the middle of the yard. There was nearly always a garrulous group of aunts, uncles, daughters and neighbours who gave us warm welcome, to the intermingled sound of cackling hens and humans. As some of our English friends living close by were also her clients, the expanded circle would often be speaking a melange of tongues: the local *patois*, my execrable Franglais, or the impeccable French of Terry and Joanna Kilmartin, while sometimes the Deffauts, with amused teasing glances in our direction, would lapse into Provençal.

They were a jolly and affectionate family, beloved alike by English and local friends. Monsieur Deffaut, who worked in some modest job for the municipality, had, during the German Occupation, used his barns as part of a chain of hiding places for getting escaping British servicemen out of France. From this he had acquired a taste for English cigarettes, and we would bring him parcels of Players when we arrived from England. He, in turn, would ply us with glasses of home-made eau de vie, sometimes of quintessential apricot

One of the olive groves on the Route de Mouriès leading down to the agricultural canal

flavour or of an odd, mysterious herbal bouquet, but always delicious if of a disconcerting potency. He would hold the liqueur glasses up to the light, so that they glowed like topaz or emerald, and smacking his lips, would wink at us in convivial pleasure.

Clearly, his war years, and the fleeting but intense friendships with escaping Allied airmen whom he sheltered, vibrated in his memory, though he did not speak in any detail about them. He was equally reticent but clear in his opinions about locals who had been less staunch than he in the Resistance. One must remember that Jean Moulin, the great Resistance leader, came from Eygalières, just across the hill, where now stand successions of milestones marked 'JEAN MOULIN, Chemin de la Liberté'. If, in one's innocence, one mentioned a local character from whom Monsieur Deffaut kept his distance, all he would say was, '*Monsieur X est très étrange*', which closed the conversation. But his evident nostalgia for the company of the Allied sevicemen who had passed through his sheltering barn was, though sometimes inarticulate, infinitely moving. The whole family had that almost Chekhovian simplicity, with its underlying strength.

By tradition, the olive harvest starts on 2 November, immediately after the religious and gastronomic festivity of *La Toussaint* (All Saints' Day). In our first season the mistral made the air quite bracing, though in others we have luxuriated through the hot day's work in rolled shirtsleeves and sun hats. Our initiation by the Deffaut family into the methods of the *récolte* proved to be a light-hearted and somehow therapeutic time of fresh air, jollity, exercise and even beauty treatment, for our hands were softened and smoothed by the emollient olives. After the indulgent feasting of *La Toussaint* we gathered in the orchard – the slim, apple-cheeked Monsieur Deffaut in his blue overalls and peaked cap, the more solid Madame D., muffled in woollens, huge knitted scarf and tea cosy hat, and their two lively daughters in flowered aprons, whose laughter echoed from among the trees.

Our small, round olive baskets, looped over the belts at our waists, left both hands free to gather the fruit, some of which, hanging on pendulous branches, can be literally sprayed into the basket as one's hands slide down, milking the laden, overhanging twigs. Each tree had to be stripped clean before the *chevalet* and paraphernalia of sacks could be moved to the next one. Any oversight was seized upon by Monsieur Deffaut as he made his final round of inspecting the tree. The lower branches at knee level were called the 'skirts', and delighted simple jokes of countrified lewdness were made if they had been neglectfully harvested. After each half-hour or so taken to fill a basket, it was a pleasant moment of let-up to stroll over and empty its contents into the large sack, standing solid with its load, between the rows of olive trees.

Later we were often helped by Marcelle Brunet, my friend of twenty-five years, who lives in Mouriès, and who in autumn drops every other activity in order to harvest, with her family, children and grandchildren, their large *terrain* of olives. Small of stature and unfailingly good-humoured of disposition, it always gave me a lift of the heart to see her arriving at Saint-Jérôme, for I knew that she would optimistically take charge, never allowing any of us to be downhearted at the size of the task before us. Whilst I would clumsily try to emulate her skill, which I greatly admired, even more did I admire her staunch felicity of temperament, and value my good luck, through the years, to have had such a friend and to have been included in her family circle.

There has recently been a change of method of *récolte*, caused by the ever rising costs of labour. Formerly only hand-picked olives were accepted at the mill, and one risked rejection of one's load if it were not impeccably free of windfalls and leaves. Both farmers and millers preserved a fierce fidelity to this orthodox style, the least departure from which was scornfully regarded as a feeble laxity of endeavour, and one's descriptions of Spanish or Italian methods provoked disapproval or derision. Now, perforce, the practice has been introduced of spreading nylon nets below and combing the trees with short-handled wooden rakes. It is certainly speedier, and thus more economical of labour, though the tree suffers many more amputations of delicate branches. Grovelling on the ground to remove the many torn branches from the nets is a far less pleasing task than gazing skywards as one gathers the rich fruit sliding through ones hands. But the new method will prevail, particularly in a good harvest year. In a lean year, like 1989, the traditional method is more effective, and we find it more enjoyable, both actively and aesthetically.

At first light of morning, the sun barely risen, getting into the swing of bending and stretching for branches low and high is invigorating, a morning's work-out, so much more natural and harmonious than that of Jane Fonda or the Muzak-driven programmes on morning television. Then, as the warmth of the sun intensifies, garments are shed, rhythm accelerates, and one's preference for the sunny side of the tree gradually wanes. As one's hands move more swiftly, gazing at the azure sky through an agitated mesh of silvery leaves and rich black fruit can be both enlivening and slightly hypnotic. When perched high upon the *chevalet*, or leaning over its apex, there can be tantalizing moments, for so often there is a most abundant branch just out of reach. But the compensations are not only the sunnier position and the larger, luscious olives to be found on high, but also the shining views over the ruffled sheen of the trees to the jagged rocks beyond.

Picking olives with the help of local friends

Madame Brunet leading the récolte

91

By four o'clock the warmth of midday begins to ebb, and soon the heavy sacks are humped and bumped over the field by wheelbarrow and slung into the boot of the car. We take the winding road through orchards, *pinède* and strange outcrops of rock to the village, where we join the lengthening queue of lorries, vans, cars, and even bicycle carts in the mill yard, by which time darkness has descended. Groups of people gather in the light of headlamps to discuss each other's progress, to peer at each other's haul, and to conjecture how many more days of picking are still before them. When our turn arrives, the olives are heaved with a roaring, rumbling sound into a giant weighing machine, through a wire mesh which traps any remaining twigs, after which they are released into the big drum below, to start their journey via moving belt and winnowing and washing machines to the *pressoir*. After the *pression à froid*, the residue is sold on to other countries, for in France it is illegal to use any oil but that of the first pressing.

A receipt for the kilos of this day's load is added to our overall tally. It is always a moment for congratulating ourselves when we first pass the 1,000-kilo mark and can casually speak of having picked a TONNE of olives. We toast this achievement in jubilation with drinks in the café. Here all is crowded, a hugger-mugger of warmth and bonhomie, jovial complaints about the weather, noisy laughter from all our farmer friends, everyone happy in the atmosphere after the last chilly hour of sundown labour. Then home we go to a luxurious bath and evening meal, soon followed by contented semi-somnolence before a log fire when, if ever one allows one's eyes to close, after-images of the long day's leafy visual field, textured like a fluctuating William Morris 'Willow Bough' design, float into view. It is a pleasure to feel attuned in body and mind, hands wonderfully soft, joints supple from the exercise, and spirits contented and composed.

In the lean years the harvest of the whole region may be finished before Christmas, and we feel a sense of urgency that unless we start promptly at *La Toussaint* the mill may have closed before we have done justice to every tree. But in the abundant or glut years the harvest may last well into the New Year. One mid-December day, the mill yard, usually so bleak and bare of all but the huge bulldozer and rattling hopper, is suddenly transformed. An avenue stretches the yard's full length, bathed in floodlighting, a wide, gleaming white pathway edged at regular intervals by large olive trees in black tubs and leading to a marquee at the far end. This is the evening of the ceremonial celebration of the olive season, followed by a party in the marquee. The seven mills of this region, renowned above all others, join in a ceremony medieval in style and even more archaic in sentiment. When, in the ceremony, the olive is cited as a symbol of peace, a moment of intensity, such as that for a well-loved prayer, passes through the crowd. The seven mills are those of Saint-Raphael, Aureille (named after the Roman Emperor on whose Via Aurelia it originally stood), Fontvieille, two in Maussane, and two in Mouriès.

First there is pageantry by people in Arlésien costume, and the priest blesses the rustic carts decorated with olive boughs. Then there is country dancing to the pipe and tabor, a

The house during a rare winter snowfall

thin, Tudor sound which lends a Shakespearian atmosphere. There are Carmarguais horse-men carrying very long lances like Don Quixote, and men on foot in long black cloaks and large floppy black hats like highwaymen. It is clear that the ladies of our region love wearing their Arlésienne dresses, and they still have the features, olive skin and Leonardo faces, which some say shows the genetic strain surviving from the original Greek settlers. Then, after a lull, a handsome young man in medieval dress, green velvet embroidered with gold, walks alone the clear length of the avenue, bearing on his shoulder a large terracotta jar of oil. With a short formal speech in the name of one of the mills, he presents it to the elderly host of the festivities, Monsieur Christian Rossi, who until he recently retired was the *patron* of our mill at Mouriès. He is the acknowledged *doyen* of the *métier*. This ritual the young man repeats another six times, amid applause, bringing oil from a different mill on each occasion. The jars, which are then arranged on a table covered with lacy white cloth like an altar, give a sense of harvest festival.

Soon the speeches become less formal; we may be treated by Monsieur Picard, a chef at the legendary local restaurant, Le Baumanière, to a special recipe in which olive oil from the region is the essential ingredient. As the solemnity of the occasion evaporates, the crowd becomes more and more convivial. We troop into the marquee, heated by braziers, and imbibe the excellent local wine, Mas Gourgonnier, a vineyard which is a few hundred yards from our house.

Of course, we had all clapped particularly hard when the oil jar from our own mill had been presented, but now, as the wine flows, our *esprit de corps* seems to expand to include our whole region, and everyone warms to a general feeling of pride in the entire locality. Delicious savouries are handed round, the decibels rise, the children darting in and out become overexcited, and it seems a good moment to leave. But the exuberance and the dancing will continue until far into the night, and on the following day in the village my Maussanois friends will tell me what a glorious festival it had been.

After the winter solstice, the Alpilles region seems to settle into a period of hibernation in tune with the dormant trees. Winter sunshine in Provence has a golden glow even on the coldest day, a glow remote from the ice-blue-grey of the North Sea climate which is but a distant memory. The landscape's colours are brilliant but evanescent, and it has a delicate beauty which the summer visitor may never see. South of Maussane, the long, immensely tall poplar windbreaks on the marshes, bare of leaves, make a ghostly glint of warm cinnamon and silver-grey against an azure sky; the mellow stucco buildings in Saint-Rémy have a radiant ochre-yellow glow against which the towering, bare plane trees cast their charcoal-coloured shadows, and the great stone arena in Arles looks paler, malleable and less forbidding than in summer. And summer's haze has given way to visibility at great distances, so that from our locality we catch unexpected glimpses of the far off Mont-Ventoux, looking like Fujiyama, or the Pic Saint Loup, way beyond Montpellier. The dramatic cliff face of the Montagne Sainte Victoire, 40 miles away near Aix-en-Provence,

*'La Follette' rose along the western
terrace wall*

Opposite: Prunus *'Okumiyako'*
(syn. P. serrulata *'Longipes') and*
Coronilla glauca

will suddenly appear, as if floating on air, as we approach the brow of our local hill – a phantom in tones of Cézanne watercolours.

Our harvest gathered, the mill fees paid, some new season's oil stowed in the car to take as Christmas presents to friends in London, and there comes the quiet time before departure when I stand in the garden, contemplating the olive trees in the field below, their thin branchlets now lighter and fluttering free. Surrounded by *maquis*, *pinède* and rocks, they form the magical foreground of our garden-in-nature, and I pause to consider how far the echoes in tone and texture in the walks we have planted are in harmony with this natural beauty. Certain plants, the teucriums, artemisias, santolinas and oleasters, take up the grey theme of the olives. The deep green of pines, junipers and holm oaks is echoed in the cypresses, mahonias and *Viburnum tinus* of the garden. The coppery tinge of the new apricot foliage is reflected in our prunus and the 'La Follette' rose. Thus far the essential consonance is not hard to achieve. However, where nature is so hard to emulate is in its character of tapestry, where splashes of colour, even of brilliance, are woven into its fabric without ever seeming to jar the senses. Yet even those plants which have naturalized in the Alpilles – for instance, *Coronilla glauca* – may seem to become more strident when brought into the garden. It may be that their garden-enriched diet elicits a floriferous riot. Yet can that be so, since they lack the years and years of leaf mould which the *maquis* has bestowed?

More likely it is that plant associations in a garden which is open to surrounding nature present a more delicate design problem than those for, say, a walled or hedged enclosure. There seems to be a running debate in one's head between the steady devotee of the natural landscape, and the more giddy enthusiast who is always tending to fall in love with the charms of a particular newly discovered plant which will, this enthusiast imagines, marry well with its companions in the border. But although the border may be well and self-sufficiently conceived in a well-chosen spectrum of colours, its relation to the surrounding Provençal *paysage* is also influenced by the harder brilliance of the Mediterranean sun. The cultivated shrubs and perennials, many brought from England, pose different and subtle problems of association in a landscape so fitfully flushed with colour.

Standing there on the brink of the olive field, my memory of the summer still vividly reflected in my mind's eye, it is often that I sense the gentle beauty of the olives rebuking me for some effect in the grey border which seems too flamboyant. For instance, an 'Apricot Nectar' rose which would in the northern English light live happily next to a coronilla, seems in Provence to render them both too assertive. I believe that under temperate English skies, away from open landscape in a walled or cottage garden, this would be a happier relationship. So it is that each year at the close of the olive season – now more than twenty years since the time of the delightful Deffauts – there are some hours spent in tranquil imaginings for the next season's gardening, contained within our affectionate, temporary goodbyes to the enchanted landscape.

The garden in May merging into the pinède

CHAPTER 7

The Greening of the Wasteland

*What would become of the garden if the gardener
treated all the weeds and slugs and birds and trespassers as he would like
to be treated, if he were in their place?*

T. H. HUXLEY, 'EVOLUTION AND ETHICS', 1893

After we were first installed in the house, quite a few years passed in dry gardening and domestic frugality until we finally acquired a more plentiful supply of water together with the electricity with which to pump it from deep underground. In the interim years we cleared thickets of gorse and blackberry, made paths, planted mainly indigenous shrubs, and continued to enjoy our quasi camping life.

We had had a disconcerting moment soon after our first week in residence. One Sunday morning, a group of farmworkers appeared with very large buckets to be filled from our well, which was at that time reluctant to satisfy our modest daily needs. We realized with not a little consternation that this must be the day of reckoning for that ominous clause in the *Acte de Vente* reserving the *droit de puisage* for the vendor, who lived in the same valley. Could this possibly become a daily occurrence, we anxiously asked ourselves? Stephen, however, having little concern for the logistics of domestic comfort, was amused. He courteously filled their buckets for them and insisted upon easing their burdens by chauffeuring them in our car back to their farm, where he invited the neighbour, their *patron*, to dine with us on the following evening.

He and his attractive wife arrived bearing a large platter of superlative fruit, for he was *expéditeur* as well as farmer. We had an enjoyable evening, and my *cuisine*, with which I had taken considerable trouble, was rather cautiously praised. This wariness I later understood when they returned the hospitality with a Sunday luncheon at the farm. We were offered the most memorable meal, superbly cooked, of which we still spoke decades later with nostalgia – crayfish *à la nage* with a superior sort of *sauce Nantua*, a *daube* of classic character, cheese from the Cévennes, and a feather-light *tarte aux pêches*. Feelings of cordiality bloomed. We realized in retrospect that the contingent of farmhands had been sent to put us to the test, and a few years later we were able to buy back the *droit de puisage*, more for our relief from nuisance than for any great boon our water could have been for them. Our peace was assured, the more so, since a member of the farmer's family was thereupon inspired to offer us the land beyond the Barberry Garden. This inspired us to work away at clearing that end of the garden for planting, though it was some years before our resources encouraged us to introduce any but the most rustic of plants for those conditions.

A few years later, one event in particular briefly raised our hopes for a verdant garden. Sitting on the terrace one early evening with our guests, Iris Murdoch and her husband John Bayley, and Barbara and Harry Weinburger, we were surprised by a visit from a water diviner, who assured us that there was a vein of water in the lower olive orchard at a depth of about seventeen metres. One by one, drinks in hand, we drifted down the slope between the trees to watch his demonstration. At a certain point in his slow, absorbed walk across the terrain the willow wand stretched taut between his hands would suddenly fly off into the air. Iris and I were impressed, though the rest of the party greeted this happening with a lofty scepticism. The diviner succeeded in persuading Stephen to try it, taking a different tack across the field, and disconcertingly the same thing happened over the same spot. '*Monsieur a le fluide*,' said the diviner with reverent enthusiasm, referring to Stephen's powers as though to some gift endowed by the Holy Ghost. Iris, too was mysteriously and powerfully gifted, and so was John, whereas I declined to be put to the test. I knew full well that were I to have tried my hand, the magic would have evaporated and our hopes petered out. The final surprise, however, was in seeing the arch-sceptic Harry being prevailed upon reluctantly to grasp the willow wand. It was clear that he consented to join the experiment only to humour us credulous creatures, and possibly assumed that his rational approach would bring us to our senses. But from his hands the divining rod made its as yet most spectacular leap.

Good scientists say that the only real test of a theory is a genuine attempt to refute it, and I see Harry as a good scientist as well as a good artist. His attitude remained detached and circumspect, for a single positive outcome gives but little support for an hypothesis, and I hesitated to ask him if his rigorous attitude had been affected, however slightly, by his experience. But subsequently a moderately decent vein of water was found at a depth of exactly seventeen metres. The flow from the well we then had dug at the spot was sufficient to top up a cistern throughout the day, and it functioned quite efficiently for six months, when the entire new well irremediably fell in. The whole enterprise ended in failure, and I am still at a loss to know what I believe about dowsing.

However, those six months of comparative plenty encouraged me to make a few new plantings. I was helped in the early mornings by Iris, who would appear silently upon the scene and take up whichever task was to hand. While the sound of John's typewriter was faintly audible from the far-off Lilac Walk, we planted, trimmed and tidied. Our conversation was sporadic, sometimes with reflective pauses between question and answer, for the

Our friends visiting Saint-Jérôme: Iris Murdoch (top), John Bayley (bottom right), David Hockney and Patrick Proctor with Stephen (centre); and, planting the Grey Walk

topic was often thought-provoking, clear rather than cryptic, yet somehow contributing to a calm atmosphere of almost Buddhist contemplation. Whilst Iris might, for instance, be engaged in illuminating points from the dialogues of Plato as she cut back the long spires of *Stachys lanata*, her loving awareness and concern for all living creatures around her was never in abeyance. It would make any gardener ashamed of murderous attitudes towards caterpillars or bumblebees. In the midst of such philosophical discourse she might inter-ject, 'I say, old thing! Take care or you might step on that little nest of ants.' One caught her compassionate attitude like an infection. These various forms of total benevolence of thought and feeling shone alike over rational quests for truth or friendly reminiscences, and made of those early-morning hours a gently amusing and refreshing interlude.

The next step, one which took us into the twentieth century, was the arrival of mains electricity. For years we had hoped that it would be brought from its nearest point, over a kilometre away, but none of our approaches to the Mairie had been successful. The Mayor of Maussane at that time was the elderly owner of the olive mill, who was a socialist. All members of our Commune, no matter what their political allegiances, respected him for his scrupulous fairness, an integral feature of his socialist principles, and he was friendly and benevolent as well as upright. His answer to our plea for a power line was to say that when the number of houses in our 'Val des Amants' reached 20 or more, the Commune would consider it worthwhile (the greatest good for the greatest number). As the Val des Amants is one of the great beauty spots of the Alpilles, which then had only a handful of old ruins or houses in rough *pierre apparente*, one of which we had restored with fidelity in the ancient style, I tentatively suggested that twenty modern houses of gleaming stucco might detract from the natural loveliness of the place. With a twinkling glance, his stern, egalitarian reply was 'Don't be selfish.' Since then, a number of modern houses have been built, some of which, with their bright villa designs and garish swimming pools, obtrude, and by their proximity to the rocks (which formerly was forbidden terrain for building) destroy the scale and grandeur of the peaks. Many people who love the Alpilles mourn the slightest intrusion to disfigure the area's untouched wildness, so that there is now beginning to be a movement to prevent further erosion of its rugged beauty.

However, unaccountably and unheralded, one summer the electricity line suddenly arrived. We enjoyed a bonanza of showering our pre-power equipment upon some as yet power-less friends. As if by telepathy (for we had had no forewarning and, being without a telephone, were relatively incommunicado), on the day that it was switched on our friend from near Uzès, Mai Zetterling, appeared on a surprise visit. She carried away in triumph the little gas refrigerator, and we did not regret the ending of our days of papal elections. A few days later Eric Idle, who had a secluded property in the wilds of the Var, relieved us of some Aladdin lamps. Our daily life was transformed; but most important of all, we could now make a serious attempt to find water, for without power this had been out of the question.

A forage was made one February day by a firm from Vitrolles, near Marseille, which

The Lilac Walk from either end with the white photinia in frothy bloom and the deep mauve lilac accidentally bought by Stephen

brought huge steel machines to the site, and unlike the little team of the diviner was much in demand by municipalities in the Vaucluse, finding water supplies for whole villages. We chose to make the attempt in the field behind our cypress windbreak, as its higher elevation would help the pressure of the flow down into the garden. As the drilling was to be paid for whether or not water was found – an expensive business, especially beyond a depth of 100 metres, when prices are doubled – I refrained from taking part as an over-anxious spectator, and retired to the Lilac Walk in my Wellington boots to do some digging. But above the rumbling and clanking of the huge machines I caught the sounds of discussions and the shouts of several people from the village who had come up the hill to watch this famous operation. Later we learned that their enthusiasm was on account of a sweepstake they were running in the village café, as to the outcome and depth of the forage. Hours passed. Then a workman ran into the garden to ask my authorization for the drilling to continue beyond 100 metres, at double the price. With some trepidation I gave my consent and returned to my digging. With a mental taximeter drumming in my head, I wondered from minute to minute at which point I should stop throwing good money after bad and acknowledge what seemed to be the dire and evident truth – that our property was a Wasteland.

Then suddenly there was a chorus of shouts from the villagers behind the trees, a whoosh over the bank behind the cypresses, and below in the Lilac Walk I was all at once standing more than calf deep in swirling water. Happily, my Wellington boots were equal to the tidal wave. Miraculous moment! Could it be true? Walking round the house and into the field, I found myself surrounded by congratulating friends from the village, laughing and preparing to rush to the café to celebrate. Yes, at 109 metres they had found an ample supply, and the technicians assured us that it was not a *poche d'eau* – a pocket backed up over the years against a subterranean rock face – but, coming from the water table, would be a reliable supply. Rash words, for in Provence water cannot be of unfailing dependability, but since then it has proved ample for our needs, despite the failure of some other wells in our valley in the exceptional drought of 1989.

It was a heady time we lived through then, daring at last to hope for the salvation of many poor plants which would no longer have to struggle to survive through *les grandes chaleurs*, when they had often failed to do so hitherto. No longer would Stephen be able to quip, in dubious taste, 'Natasha runs a concentration camp for flowers.' Many of my heart's desires could now be welcomed into a dwelling place more congenial to them. Where should we begin?

Naturally, we were drawn to the point which had seen the original attempts to realize the grand design, close to home on the terrace and then in the Lilac Walk. By this time we had started another cypress hedge on the walk's south side, which we had intended to keep at a height of two metres, so that it would enclose the walk whilst admitting enough sunshine. However, there was almost total insurrection from the trees. They refused to be restrained,

Euphorbia characias *(above);*
the 'Lord Selborne' tree paeony and
the black tulips which surround it in the pink
border (above right and detail)

and we were obliged first to thin them to admit shafts of sunlight between the trunks, and then to allow them to grow to their natural loftiness. In front of them were the enticing spaces between the more drought-tolerant shrubs, and this invitation to plant quite went to our heads.

At that time, a passionate interest of the moment was the display of tree paeonies we had seen at Kelways. Since paeonies had done so well for Sir Frederick Stern in his chalk garden at Highdown, might they also thrive in our strongly alkaline conditions? Indeed they do. The 'Duchess of Kent' lives at the foot of *Rosa* 'La Follette' on the terrace, and the pure white 'Mrs William Kelway' spreads herself at the near end of the Lilac Walk. They are both generous in bloom, sometimes quite bowed down at the zenith of their opulent season. At first we felt restrained from indulging our hankering for paeonies throughout the garden, since the brevity of their flowering means that there are long, less colourful months of summer to follow. Even so, with such elegant foliage persisting into autumn, they more than warrant their favoured position in the borders.

Soon the paler 'Lord Selborne' was planted in the pink border, where in some years its most floriferous time coincides with the screen of apple blossom behind it. We have surrounded it with black tulips, 'Sable Night' iris, and a crowd of *Euphorbia characias*. Near them, some herbaceous paeonies are equally free of their favours; they are jolly, shocking-pink ones, bought locally, which follow a little later and scramble against the more ethereal beauty bush (*Kolkwitzia amabilis*). In the Lilac Walk there is a large clump of

The ethereal Kolkwitzia amabilis

The grey border with, in the foreground,
cerastium, lavender stoechas, centranthus alba
and artemesia

'Duchesse de Nemours', which prolongs the paeony season after 'Mrs William Kelway' is on the wane.

The Mediterranean is the natural habitat of several species paeonies, all single flowered, and it has long been my desire to collect some into the congenial surroundings with which, I believe, we can provide them. However, until very recently I have been unable to find a nursery supply, and we regard collecting from the wild as absolutely taboo. Though I have not been there recently, there is a high valley in the Hérault beyond Montpellier where we saw large clumps of *Paeonia peregrina* spread over the ground (at least, that was the name given to it by a local enthusiast). *Paeonia humilis* comes from Spain, as does *P. broteroi*, though in each case they are happiest in woodland and mountain sites more elevated than we can offer them. More desirable than their crimson blooms which are the parents of so many cultivated varieties, would be the Cretan *P. clusii* and *P. rhodia* from Rhodes, both islands with hot, dry summers and rainy winters. They both have ballooning, white single flowers, with stamens of a rich yellow. However, we have had to wait for many years before we could find and accommodate the many members of the paeony family which we then imagined would take kindly to us.

Our next enthusiasm was for rugosa roses. As soon as the earth was no longer cement-hard in summer, a 'Blanche Double de Coubert', which had previously clung rather miserably to life in the Lilac Walk, now enjoyed a glorious revival. Elsewhere we planted *R. rugosa* 'Alba', which immediately flourished, and we were particularly taken by a bush of 'Scabrosa' with its vivid cerise flowers and soft, yellow anthers. Both its flowers and, later, the tubby hips make a lively contrast to the deep green foliage. The little 'Schneezwerg' had been our original introduction to rugosas, and it had been happy from our very first planting on the terrace, where it looked charmingly demure alongside the more grandiose gesture of 'La Follette'.

That first summer of the rehydration of the Wasteland also encouraged us to try new varieties of *Hibiscus syriacus*. In Provence we had been able to find only a blue one, and the white variety with a central blotch of crimson, neither of which were more specifically named. They had languished in the drought, but soon took on a new lease of life when

The garden in its early days; a rare year when
the Meadow Garden was scarlet
with poppies (opposite the Grey Walk); Natasha
and Stephen's newly-built fish pond; and the
Cotinus coggygria *in the Barberry Walk*

water had arrived. We brought in the pale orchid-pink 'Ardens', and the pure white crinkly 'Diana' found a home in the new Grey Walk which at last we were able to begin to plant.

Hitherto the western end of the garden had perforce remained comparatively wild, but now we were encouraged to begin a whirlwind operation of clearing the indigenous scrub of gorse and blackberry which had encroached from the hillside when little else could tolerate our meagre hospitality. The best of the native growth was retained, including a huge old pine tree and a wild pear, together with some elder and cistus. The prospect of planting around them seemed like painting a picture on a canvas already splashed with colour which had to be incorporated into the composition. We renamed this bronze walk 'Barberry', for the most successful of the shrubs we had already established there. The pomegranate hedge was doing well, and the arbutus and purple-leaved maple grew quite tall. For the immediate season we were able to add *Rosa glauca* and *Cotinus coggygria*, leaving the foreground bare to be designed and planted in a subsequent year.

But the greatest impetus to action centred on the enclosed garden. Hitherto it had been a totally neglected patch of thistles, weeds and couch grass, though rejoicing in springtime with wild muscari of a most celestial blue, and later in the summer with *Verbascum longi-folium*. It seemed wanton to think of eradicating the muscari, so we tried to transplant them to the southern edge of the garden, which we wished to assume a meadow character to blend with the olive orchard below. But nature insists on going its own way. Although this 'meadow' will one year be flushed golden with tiny marigolds and later scarlet with poppies, or in another year be surging with elegant grasses and the luminous echinops, it seemed to resist any of our purposeful additions. The muscari continually elect to appear only on the otherwise pristine gravel paths, and any amount of delving and transplanting seems ineffective in discouraging them. A rosemary hedge was planted round the edge of this central rectangle, now to become the Rose Garden, and four paths edged with box were made to converge upon a circle at the centre.

Then we were struck with a hitherto unthinkably bold idea. Why shouldn't Stephen, after many years of imagining the impossible, realize his dream of a fountain and fishpond? A simple circular pond was soon made, its parapet standing knee-high above the ground, with a wide, flat sill on which one can sit and watch the goldfish gliding between the water lilies. Wherever one may be in the garden, the sound of the fountain mingling with that of the cicadas echoing from the hillside induces a sense of Oriental calm.

Since we often like to pause and reflect as we stroll round the garden we decided to place some stone benches at intervals, one midway down the Lilac Walk, and another at the far side of the Mycenaean corner. Here one may gaze ahead upon the length of the walk towards the house, or south through the bronzy tones of Barberry towards the rocks. A third, beneath a holm oak on an elevated knoll above the olive orchard, is known as 'Granny's Bench'. My mother had often chosen that spot for contemplating the rocks when, in her eighties, she made her annual visit. In early life, after her childhood emigration from Russia, she had been an actress in the Old Vic company during and after the First World War. Half a century later, overtaken by deafness, her remarkable interpretive gifts had ceded place to creative ones. In her late seventies, with her customary concentration, she had suddenly and with success taken to painting, which gave her an intense pleasure. Her vision seemed to be like a Russian Expressionism giving voice to the pure simplicity of a Grandma Moses. Staying at Saint-Jérôme, she would spend the entire day at her easel, and after a certain interval, we would take her a picnic basket, and sit admiring her work and chatting about the landscape she regarded as entirely her own. She saw the rocks as indomitable personalities, 'Roman Sentinels', and would never tire of absorbing herself in every facet of their characters. Beneath the holm oak was one of her favoured vantage points (another down the lane is still known as 'Granny's Glade'), and later, feeling that her spirit still hovers there, we cleared a spot for a stone bench carved with her initials. This last addition completed the architectural plan of the garden.

For the first time since we had acquired the terrain, the cultivation was extended beyond my capacity as an absentee gardener to give the plants the attention they need at the appropriate season. Missing the early months of the year, when feeding and pruning would have been easily accomplished had I been in residence, meant also that the vital time for early weeding would be long past when I arrived for the Easter holidays. In Provence, the spring being so much earlier than it is in England, it is imperative to get at the annual weeds before they can seed themselves, laying up trouble for subsequent years.

On the long springtime drive from England I would, in sunny anticipation, picture the garden in its luxuriant, impeccable state of the previous summer. Invariably I would arrive to a disheartening, even overwhelming, confusion. The affectionate leap of the heart as we turned into the driveway after many hours of travelling was quickly followed by sad concern at the atmosphere of neglect. The penalty for having the joy of a continuity with the *maquis* in our immediate view is that it showers us with its seedlings. By April, huge onopordum thistles with prickly, marbled leaves, their seeds having been wafted in from the surrounding wilderness, waxed tall and abundant; the fleshy tuber-like roots of the couch grass had enjoyed an underground winter of content and were sending up fresh green growth; the docks were crowding in; and newly seeded brambles were full of vitality. The treasures brought with me from England would sit patiently waiting in a corner of the terrace until their new, permanent home could be swept and garnered so as to be worthy of them.

It is as well to learn a certain discipline of mind and spirit in the face of such a mammoth task looming before one. Despair must be repudiated, and one must resolve to close one's eyes to every region of the garden but the one selected for the day's endeavour. Often one catches sight of a pressing need for elementary care elsewhere in the garden – perhaps a certain shrub may importune and pathetically plead to be attended to out of turn. It is heartrending, but one must stay with the task in hand, for unless a considerable area of

Granny's bench beneath the holm oak, overlooking the olive groves and the 'Roman Sentinel' rocks

Granny's painting, the view from her favoured vantage point

friendly old shrubs and climbers is restored to wellbeing and left nodding its appreciation, the general reproach emanating from the other languishing beauties becomes too hard to bear. 'Your turn tomorrow' is murmured to them at the end of a day. Yet the delay imposed upon the newcomers from England can be less than kind, since they need the precious weeks to get established before the onslaught of *les grandes chaleurs*. A counsel of perfection would require all planting to occur in the autumn months. Yet it is seldom possible to resist the springtime afterthoughts, held in abeyance from gardening inspirations and resolutions of the previous olive-picking visit, when the demands of harvesting are too great to allow of any other activity.

The spring-cleaning task has become far less onerous since the garden has matured and my methods have improved; happily so, since it remains a 'one-pair-of-hands' garden. The cypress windbreak has grown tall enough to impede a great many of the seeds flying in from the field beyond, and the shrubs and ground cover have spread themselves to make us less hospitable to those which do win through. Yet how inconsistent, even emotional, one can be towards which of these airborne intruders may find a welcome. In England, I have often seen in the most admirable of gardens groups of onopordums, proudly labelled and lovingly tended. Perhaps we, too, should offer them temporary accommodation for the shining beauty of their sculptured foliage. I don't deny that they can be magnificent, but having for so long regarded them as more pernicious than the Boston Strangler, even pre-serving them in a state of childlessness would not endear them to us. Some flowering weeds behave with a becoming discretion, filling bare corners with a shy flush of colour, and politely enhancing their cultivated neighbours. But the onopordums are a greedy crowd who jostle every other resident to yield them the place to which they lay claim. Fortunately, in common with other bullies, and given that one has a stout pair of gloves in which to attack them, they quickly prove unequal to the contest and are counted out.

By contrast, two native species to find a warm welcome in our garden, one wafted in and one planted, are euphorbia and valerian (*Centranthus ruber*, both red- and white-flowered forms). This evokes astonishment from local friends who find our choice eccentric, if not ruinous to the general effect. 'Why have you planted the border with weeds?' asks the postman or the plumber. Monsieur Gilles, a local and for a short time a sporadic helper in the garden, used to put on a mournful face whilst I would extol their qualities, and then shrug his shoulders in reply, '*Oh, comme vous voulez, c'est à vous!*' Yet both species associate particularly well with our cultivated shrubs and bulbs. *Euphorbia characias*, after its spring season of exotic green-black flower heads, has such rich whorls of foliage, and *Centranthus ruber* gives such a smoky red glow through its long summer of bloom, that each has proved

View towards the Grey Walk from Granny's bench with iris and yellow broom in the foreground

invaluable. Moreover, their softer tones both enhance and intervene between, competing cultivated plants of more jubilant hue.

We usually arrived for our annual four-month residence after the best moment of spring bulbs, which I have disposed in the garden to give maximum pleasure when, on the coldest days, we look out from the windows of the house. Our friends who delight in house-sitting during the winter give us lyrical descriptions when we arrive to take over at the end of March, and there have been some years when we have been able to see for ourselves on a February visit. Gazing through the windows of a warm room may sound like craven unwillingness to brave the elements, but there can be days of brilliant winter sun when the mistral bites and buffets so mercilessly that there is no possibility of standing outdoors to contemplate. Rather, one must lean up against the wind, as if it were the strongest of ocean currents, and resolutely fight one's way to shelter. On those days, when the house creaks and strains like a ship at sea, it is a joy to look from indoors at those crowded patches of spring colour, each bloom bravely trembling in the wind's onslaught. Again, it is the Provençal light which endows the flowers with a character different from their kind in England, and their colours being yet more brilliant leads to a search for softer tones with which to mingle them.

Of course, even in those halcyon first years after the arrival of water we were to have failures. The education of a gardener is certainly a lifelong process for 'mature students'. No less than three times I gave valuable, partly shaded wall space to *Hydrangea petiolaris*, and at each attempt I gave it lashings of compost, acid *terreau*, and watered it devotedly. 'It won't do', gloomed one of my experienced gardening friends in the Vaucluse, who had also unsuccessfully tried it a number of times. Probably it disliked not only the dry Mediterranean heat, but also the wind, for the only local success I have seen with this ravishing climber is in an enclosed garden in Tarascon. Here, with walls more than four stories high, the wind does not penetrate, moisture is retained even in the hottest weather, and both foliage and flowers are superb. But it is fair to say that my friends who have recently created this exceptional garden, which I shall later describe in more detail, are not only devoted but inspired when choosing for their special micro-climate.

Scarcely less reluctant, but nevertheless surviving, has been *Fremontodendron californicum*. Considering its American West Coast provenance it might be expected, like its compatriot ceanothus, to thrive in our Mediterranean conditions. Yet although for me it produces its charming flowers in due season, for a great many years it resolutely refused to grow above three feet or so. There is always the chance that it disliked the site, being perhaps stunted by a soil deficiency close to the house wall. Francoise Giraud, who used to run the best local nursery, Les Jardins de Provence at Saint-Rémy, and who is certainly more green-fingered than I, mourns a similar lack of success with fremontodendron. It could be that our summers are too dry compared to the humidity of the Pacific coast, or indeed of England, although it grows well here in part-shade under the limitless automatic

The Fremontodendron californicum, *a present from a gardening friend*

watering in a neighbour's *domaine*. But when, leaning out of an upper window of South Cottage in the Sissinghurst garden, I see it almost touching the eaves in happy association with a rose, 'Madame Alfred Carrière', I can hardly overcome the wistfulness which accompanies my enjoyment there of its evident wellbeing. One of its great virtues, to my mind, is the mellow ochre colour of its petals as they die, still clinging to the branches. Were it to offer only a strident gold against the deep green, its impact would be far less attractive than that of its dappled mosaic of chrome-and-amber, buff and a pure butter-yellow, all set against the glossy, dark, trefoil-shaped foliage. It is *nuancée* as well as brilliant.

A kind neighbour offered me a flourishing fremontodendron, which for aesthetic reasons could no longer occupy its site, now charmingly composed of pale blues and pinks. We were both seized with enthusiasm to think of its migration to Saint-Jérôme, for no aspiring parent could be keener to adopt a homeless child than I to offer this plant a new abode. But prudence had to prevail, and the move awaited the dormant season. Moreover, in view of my previous partial failure, could I possibly offer it a worthy, equally pampered habitat? Heart-searchings on this score alternated with the welling feelings of hospitality towards this immigrant young beauty, coming from a hitherto sheltered existence. As for humans, so for plants – the heredity-versus-environment debate and its train of conjectures occupy the mind. Whether an individual proves tough or tender must always come down to an intricate interaction between nature and nurture. One is forever balancing experience and prediction against the hazards of climate and conditions, forever reconciling the celebration of successes with the mourning of losses. But after an anxious winter, we were overjoyed when the foster child seemed happy.

As this garden approaches its coming-of-age and I have survived past the golden years, a busy yet contented feeling assails me of being like 'the old woman who lived in a shoe' towards my plants. As some mature sufficiently to look after themselves more easily, the newcomers, like new children, receive a larger share of loving care, as well as being sheltered by the older, more robust members of the garden family. Yet as plants come and go among the longer-lived survivors – the main scheme being perennial, although its details may change – we are put in mind of the repaintings of old pictures, the previous underlying versions of which are discovered by art historians with their X-ray machines. I am certainly no master, though for creating a garden, intentions, and their fulfilment, remain a woven strand of visual memory, even if some features can no longer be remembered unless their former felicity is a cause for present regret.

Certain changes are forced upon one when the site suddenly appears to go on strike. This happened when my beloved ceanothus was whipped right out of the ground by a mistral, and subsequent replacements have been repudiated by that patch of soil. I was disposed to blame my ignorance, for I remain *amateur* in this highly professional *métier*. But my consolation is that it can occur even in the most renowned and well-conducted gardens. Most memorable was the lively charm of the Sissinghurst nuttery in its original underplanting of polyanthus in all hues, brilliant flashing colours like the gleam of faceted precious stones, with the fresh green hazel foliage overhead. But after Vita Sackville-West's time the soil went on the most obdurate strike, which proved irreversible for polyanthus, whatever scientific analysis was studied. It is now underplanted with an undulating carpet of soft colours and textures which has its own allure, although the former character is still a treasured memory.

The changes at Saint-Jérôme have not only been provoked by demands of soil and climate, and my expanding enthusiasms, for some were the fruit of my having profited from the growing expertise of many friends who have recently created gardens in the region. Naturally those living close at hand in the Alpilles share more of the prevailing conditions, but even those living in the Vaucluse or on the slopes of Mont-Ventoux have much experience to exchange, advice to give and take, appreciations to share. The warmth and enjoyment of this circle, like an informal fraternity, is among the greatest pleasures of living in Provence.

View into the mature garden from Iberia, the native holm oaks and pines in the background

The Henri IV façade at the Château de Saint-Estève

CHAPTER 8

Gardening Friendships

*The great round white pitted rock, now seemed to hang there
like a vast heroic shield*

IRIS MURDOCH, 'NUNS AND SOLDIERS', 1980

When first we settled at Saint-Jérôme, inevitably many of our friends in the region were English, and although they shared our passion for the captivating French countryside and style, they were far from having been born to it. It was often easier to seek advice from those who had recently passed through the heady phase of discovery, than from French friends who, though willing, were from lifelong familiarity far less able to see quite how amazingly different things might be from our previous experience. Staying in 1964, as in a haven, with Anne and Rodrigo Moynihan, already established in their Domaine de Saint-Estève in the Aixois country near Lambesc, we used to feel both refugee from the heat and dust of our building operations, and tenderfoot in the ways of Provence.

On an inauspiciously rainy September day, five years earlier, Anne and Rodrigo had discovered the ruined château standing in its 90 hectares of neglected land. They had first come upon the vast and desolate walled kitchen garden near the farm buildings, in the centre of which there was a large rectangular stone cistern with a running fountain shaded by a spreading lime tree. Already they were possessed by an atmosphere of former glory in this benign decaying estate, as if they would at any moment come upon '*Le Grand Meaulnes*'. The fields immediately surrounding the walled garden had already been harvested of their melons and artichokes, whilst a late planting of carrots and spinach was beginning to show. As they wandered on their soggy way, huddled under a large umbrella, the land around them seemed both ineptly commercialized yet forlornly romantic.

Five hundred yards to the south stood the ruins of the château, only the ground-floor rooms still standing behind the grand Henri IV façade, for the top floors had collapsed in the earthquake of 1909. The ground floor had been roofed over by the farmer, and horribly partitioned into very small rooms behind the noble windows, but the Moynihans had at once seen that the original proportions would be recoverable. Adjoining the château was an earlier wing, and the wall of an ancient chapel. In spite of the evident vastness of the task of restoring the whole agglomeration of ruined land and buildings, the couple had felt irresistibly drawn to undertake it, not least for the very large spaces it afforded for their respective studios.

When we visited five years later, the château had regained its seventeenth-century character, roofed now at the top level of the beautiful northern façade, its august proportions regained throughout, and the southern elevation having, above the tall windows, a more informal, almost farmhouse aspect. Where Anne and Rodrigo created an exceptional charm of ambience was in blending throughout the *domaine* these two elements, the noble formality with the farmhouse character. On an axis with the central horseshoe staircase of the classic north façade they had planted, with admirable faith in the future, an avenue of pale poplars leading out to the farm buildings with their walled garden. Being amply watered by small canals, the avenue now forms a very high, glinting, rustling corridor, giving a sense of a more northern French *paysage* – as it might be, the Loire. On the south side of the house, a courtyard within high walls fronts the long, low dining room, previously the cellars of the château, where the shapes of the traditional '*arcade*' stone vaulting are delineated by corresponding *demi-lune* windows which the Moynihans designed. In summer we would sit in the fig tree's deep shade in this courtyard, surrounded by pots of scented geraniums, jasmine, amaryllis, and by giant buddleias and the richly coloured *vigne vierge* lapping to a great height upon the walls. The first lesson for the tenderfoot in Provence is the need for shade close to the house. Very often, as in the Deffauts' farmyard, it may be provided by an ancient fig tree, or by the huge plane trees pruned to a flattened parasol shape which may so often be seen standing before an old *mas*. Thus a large pool of shade is created which may extend to the iron pergola jutting from the house, which is usually covered by a vine of cardinal grapes, or a trumpeting bignonia, or sometimes a wisteria, and under which stand pots of brilliantly coloured flowers. We speedily learned our first lesson.

Beyond the château's shaded courtyard, below some magnificent ancient plane trees growing unpruned and to their natural height, the neglected *terrain* of farmyard rubble was transformed into lawns sloping towards the vineyards. In the shade of these giant trees near the house they made large rectangular stone *bassins* with wide sills at knee level and ancient lion-headed fountains, each constantly spewing a thread of water. It seemed incredible that after only a year the *bassins* seemed as weathered as the house, for Rodrigo had speeded the process from the *fromage blanc* gleam of the new-cut stone by lacing pails of water with some Indian ink and, as he said, 'sloshing it over them'. The result was an apparent antiquity of garden ornament, seeming similar in age and proportion to the great plane trees. At Saint-Jérôme, we were tempted to take to 'sloshing' in our impatience with

At Saint-Estève: The avenue of pale poplars; ancient plane trees; a gargoyle within the horseshoe staircase

*Rodrigo Moynihan and the portrait he
painted of his wife, Anne Dunn*

the too white *pierre de Fontvieille*, but our procrastination gave nature its chance, and within two or three years the terraces, steps and garden seats mellowed.

The grand expanses of Saint-Estève do not seem to invite flower gardening as such, particularly on the north side, where the noble façade, partly clad in a dark creeper, enjoys the sobriety of dark green evergreens shadowed by a few tall trees. But on the more informal south side, long narrow borders skirting the straight drive alongside the courtyard are planted with a harlequin succession of coloured shrubs, perennials and annuals, with a lively felicity which only a painter's eye can achieve. Every year there are minor variations, but always an air of happy improvisation, like a quick sketch dashed off in a morning capturing the moment, which seems the antithesis of deliberate garden design. Like the gardens of Cedric Morris, or even the magical Giverny, there is no hint of explicit theory of colour, but rather the instinctive associations which make one feel charmed and carefree. I am reminded of this gift, having watched Rodrigo painting a portrait in his large studio under the eaves. He would give a darting glance at the sitter, then remain poised for a moment before adding a small and brilliant accent which often seemed to revive movement and light in a previously static area of the painting. As a devotee, myself, of a harmonious but restricted palette in planting the borders, I nevertheless caught the inspiration from Saint-Estève of the whimsical touches of opposite colour which enliven and even intensify the effect of the main theme.

When we had first arrived in Provence, the variety and character of fresh vegetables in the local street markets had been a delectable discovery. Nothing can equal the savour and bloom of the piles of freshly gathered, shining aubergines, tomatoes, *haricots verts*, and courgettes with their delicate yellow flowers, unless they be surpassed by those culled from a *potager* an hour or so before they are to be eaten. Our aspirations were long centred on making a kitchen garden, but we regretfully realized that this dream would have to wait until we could live the year round in Provence. Meanwhile, the glowing vegetables lying in large *panniers* and brought into the cool farmhouse kitchen at Saint-Estève shortly before a meal, then in winter eaten at the long wooden table set before its charcoal fire, led us to study the new *potager* the Moynihans had made and to store up observations against the time when eventually we might emulate it.

High cypress hedges on three sides protected this *potager* from the fierce winds, while on the south it was entirely open to the sun even when, at the winter solstice, the sun is at its lowest above the horizon beyond the low-growing vines. The rotation of crops was admirably managed, and after an initial resistance the gardener took to Anne's innovations. For instance, she imported good American strains of seed for sweetcorn, which was hitherto despised locally as food fit only for poultry, or at best for the rustic, polenta style dishes made from dried corn. Twenty years later, fresh corn on the cob is at last becoming available – and popular – in local markets. But there are also many vegetable species belonging to this region and unequalled elsewhere – the swollen spheres of garlic with fat fleshy cloves which are easily crushed, the strong-flavoured sorrel, the rocket for salads, and the small 'violet' artichokes, so tender even when raw. Strawberries are particularly good in Provence, and even though raspberries are more difficult in this climate, the ones at Saint-Estève are delicious, possibly because the canes brought from England also thrive in more winter frost than can occur further south.

Gradually we began gathering advice and local lore. We soon found that the rubrics governing the planting and tending of vegetables were followed with a rigid fidelity and were usually related to the calendar of saints' days or the phases of the moon. However, they seem to vary from region to region, which is scarcely surprising since the variations in local climate have turned out to be more pronounced than might have been expected, even within the Bouches-du-Rhône and the neighbouring *départements* of the Gard, the Hérault and the Vaucluse. This is largely due to the comparative influence of the mistral, which is at its greatest in the hinterland between Hyères and Fos-sur-Mer, due south of Saint-Jérôme. The spreading funnel effect gives it less and less influence further east until at the Côte d'Azur the protection offered by the Alpes Maritimes makes the possibility of frost a very rare one. Similarly, to the west, from the Camargue to Perpignan, the mistral yields to the *cers Languedocien* and the *tramontane du Roussillon* until the shelter of the Pyrenées gives the mildest of climates to the coast around Collioure. But surprisingly there is even a great difference between the north and south of our little range of the Alpilles, the plain just to its north from Tarascon to Orgon having noticeably colder winter weather. Thus, even the advice we sought from Saint-Estève was to be modified by what we could learn locally in our own valley.

Our nearest neighbours at that time were but a mile away at the Mas des Calans, which we used to pass every day on our way to the village, glimpsing as we drove by the gates a garden which seemed luxuriant and mature, though later in the sixties, when we had become friends with its owners, we learned how recently it had been created. Afterwards, in the early eighties, our friends Yves Coutarel and Bobbie Parkinson moved on to Tarascon, and now a tall, solid gate obscures what had always been *en passant* a pleasant, mysterious glimpse as we drove to the village.

For a namesake housewarming present, I gave Bobbie and Yves a 'Bobbie James' rose brought from England when they moved from Mas des Calans to their newly restored house in Tarascon. There it has long rampaged up four tall storeys in a courtyard garden, cascading a profusion of white blooms from roof to mezzanine in ghostly glory. Theirs is the most spectacular example, but although hitherto unknown in this region the rose is now beginning to appear in many local gardens from cuttings given by the generous Bobbie and Yves, and propagated for enthusiastic recipients by local nurseries. Style is changing in some gardens of Western Provence. Garish colours have become less popular; gradually a wider range of cultivars is becoming available; gardens are acquiring more individuality. Sometimes the passion for a hitherto unknown plant may spread like wildfire

The 'Bobbie James' rose given as a housewarming present to our friends Bobbie and Yves

Preparing for aquatic sports in the agricultural canal (opposite)

over a huge region, as when Bobbie, visiting us at Sissinghurst, fell deeply in love with *Osteospermum* 'Whirlygig', and took a plant back to a Tarascon nurseryman. Now, but a few years later, it has spread over six surrounding *départements*. This change in style is partly due to the charm of some English gardens in the region, and partly to the influence of Yves Coutarel who, as *Chef de Culture* for the town of Tarascon, and in collaboration with the municipal head of gardening, Georges Grillet, has created public gardens of unusual beauty. They also developed the annual festival, the Tarascon Floralies, where exhibitors ranging from the Pyrenées to the Côte d'Azur give great delight to the local gardening public, as well as exchanging ideas with each other.

But when we first made friends with Bobbie and Yves they had only recently restored their Mas des Calans, near Maussane, with its traditional vaulted rooms, and with its stone barns and outside staircase all shaded by Chinese mulberry trees. They transformed the farmyard, previously consisting of neglected chicken runs on arid earth, into a garden of meandering grassy paths and beautiful bushes and trees, the terrain crisscrossed with little channels of running water, for they had the good fortune to have the agricultural canal at their front gate.

Long ago, in the sixteenth century, a public-spirited and highly competent hydraulic engineer, Adam de Craponne, conceived a scheme of supplying water for the whole region surrounding his native Salon-de-Provence by canals which were fed by the river Durance. Amazingly, given the rudimentary technical resources in that century, his colossal scheme was completed in only five years. On 20 April 1559, the clergy and the entire population assembled for the ceremony of blessing the arrival of the water. Indeed it was blessed, for 'le canal de Craponne' transformed the agriculture of the whole region so successfully that to this day the area is called 'the Garden of France'. It was later elaborated to serve quite small communities, and in this the Vallée des Baux owes much to the work of Paul Revoil, who is gratefully commemorated by a plaque on the wall of the church in Maussane.

In the Alpilles the canal flows quite fast in its winding course, running in wide channels which branch into smaller ones. Coming from Aureille to the east of us the water rushes along our valley – alas some 600 metres distant from and below Mas Saint-Jérôme, too far for our land to profit from it. Soon after flowing under the bridge of our little road which leads to Mouriès, the water tumbles noisily over some rapids, then surges round a bend to a long straight stretch along the south side of the rocky ridge. Suddenly it disappears into a dark tunnel through the ridge at right angles to it, emerging on the north side to wind gently through the fields and hamlet of Les Calans. On their annual visits, Iris Murdoch and John Bayley have always been fascinated by the canal and its changes of character; indeed, with its rather satanic long tunnel, it figures dramatically in Iris's novel *Nuns and Soldiers*. More recently, other guests of ours have followed the Bayleys' lead in inventing enjoyable aquatic sports in the canal, and the valley sometimes echoes with the cheers of less adventurous guests who stand on the bank enjoying the sight of their friends whizzing by in the swift current. I have seen youths from the village plunging down the rapids and speeding towards the tunnel, their only gear being two pairs of blue jeans. At the end of their sporting journey they peel off the sodden outside pair and stroll away in the immaculate, bone-dry inner one.

At Mas des Calans in the evening, Bobbie would lift a trapdoor by his front gate and the water would come gushing into the labyrinth of little channels devised to course through every foot of their imperceptibly south-sloping garden. This system resembles that of the ancient Romans, still partly extant and in daily use in a few properties near Glanum on the north side of the Alpilles. With this inestimable boon, a miraculously mature garden was achieved at Mas des Calans in very few years. The other vestiges of the former farmyard were a fig tree shading the outside staircase and bearing the most luscious black fruit, a very old almond near the entrance under which they planted scilla and early ornithogalum to enhance the ethereal spring blossom, and an even more ancient silkworm mulberry, hollow almost to the base, and inhabited by a large white owl and a fat brown toad. All else was planted by Bobbie and Yves who, like us, were new to Provençal gardening, their previous know-how deriving from their experiences in their earlier home in the more sub-Alpine climate of eastern Alsace.

We all found ourselves, sometimes through mini-disasters, learning the inappropriateness of northern methods. But since Mas des Calans had been started a few years earlier than Mas Saint-Jérôme, I was far more often led than leader in learning Provençal ways. For instance, with due permission, Bobbie had transplanted some young pine trees taken from the overcrowded maquis to form a windbreak against the mistral. Unfortunately ten out of twelve saplings had perished, and later, while seeking replacements, he met an elderly inhabitant walking his dog, who perceived the task in hand and said, 'Of course, you have brought your chalk!'

'Chalk?' enquired Bobbie in some astonishment.

'But naturally,' the old man replied, 'you must mark with chalk the side of the tree facing towards the mistral, and you must plant it in the same orientation in which it has learned to withstand nature.' All the pine trees of the second planting survived to form an effective shelter for the garden.

Being both painters and designers of textiles, posters and fashions, Bobbie and Yves were never for a moment without some immediate project to fulfil. Thus life at Les Calans was crammed with creative work, interspersed with leisurely meals and sauntering garden strolls. Whether professional work with its impending deadlines, a favour or present for a friend, or an amateur pursuit for their own pleasure, their intense enjoyable commitment to the task in hand was total. One summer I taught Yves, who in practice had no previous musical experience, to play Bach and Schumann on the piano, and in return he taught me to make Provençal dishes like the historically authentic Marseillaise bouillabaisse.

This lightning operation began with a high-speed dash into Saint-Rémy-de-Provence,

Stephen, Bobbie (also below), Yves and I seated in front of the trough

The 'Canary Bird' shrub rose (right), one of my English imports

arriving precisely at *midi* when the morning's catch, sparkling fresh, was hastily delivered to the fishmonger by a Marseillais fisherman from his dilapidated car. Then, having bought fish, we drove equally fast to Les Calans, where a large cauldron of water was already on the boil in readiness. There was no nonsense permitted about adding later, heretical ingredients like lobster to the traditional recipe. Only the original Mediterranean fish were used, *rascasse*, monkfish, eel, and *Saint-Pierre*, with numerous small rockfish and some menacing looking weevers. The sweated onions, tomatoes and olive oil, the herbs and saffron were flung in, followed by the fish, and while they simmered, the garlic croutons and the hot *rouille* were prepared. Within an hour of our setting out for Saint-Rémy we would be sitting at table on the terrace under the Chinese mulberry tree, the delicate scent of jasmine mingling with the rich, rock-pool aroma of the bouillabaisse.

From this terrace one faced an inviting, narrow alley of cypresses leading due south, its deep shade illuminated from below by the brilliant vermilion of 'Super Star' roses, their dewy luminance enlivened by their setting in shadow. Emerging into sunlight at the cypress tunnel's end, one was presented with a choice of winding grassy paths through seemingly unlimited space, though all ways led ultimately back to the house. Shrubs which do particularly well in the Alpilles, *Abelia grandiflora*, *Cistus ladanifer*, oleanders, were set in large clumps to provide great splashes of colour, with the smaller drifts of perennials, bulbs and annuals making a more mosaic effect below them. With no straight vistas here, the herbaceous treasures were often come upon with an element of surprise. At the far southern end of this painterly, Impressionist garden one gazed back beyond the low house at a monumental outcrop of limestone rock standing sentinel above the lush, aromatic foreground of the garden.

Each of us was in the habit of conceiving sudden passions for particular plants, passions which would blow up suddenly like flurries of mistral, clamouring to be shared. Introducing friends to one's latest obsession was a thrilling moment, tinged with suspense; would it receive the perceptive welcome it deserved? From England I brought tree paeonies ('Duchess of Kent', 'Duchess of Marlborough') and shrub roses (*R*. 'Geranium', 'Canary Bird') which grew exuberantly in their well-tended habitat at Mas des Calans and received the acclamation I had hoped for. Bobbie and Yves gave me a hardy datura of purest white which didn't seem to languish in my then drought-ridden terrain. One year, Yves's passion was exclusively for a spectacular echium from the Côte d'Azur, which he managed to cherish in a sheltered spot in the more rugged Alpilles climate, although roughing it at the even more exposed Mas Saint-Jérôme was not to be thought of. Then Bobbie discovered that *Coronilla glauca* had naturalized extravagantly in the wild, and bringing it into the garden became the dominant enthusiasm of that year. He gave it to Robert and Odette Faye at Mas de la Dame, the vineyard at the foot of Les Baux, where it is tailored into elegant golden spheres. But we gave it freedom, used it as host to later-flowering viticella clematis, and even rejoiced in its unruliness. Now I find it a shade too

The lily pond on the ground level of the terrace at rue de l'Amoureux and the Magnolia grandiflora 'Exmouth' an exotic addition to the garden

brilliant, and favour *Coronilla* 'Citrina' which is, however, regrettably less robust than its cousin.

I have not seen Mas des Calans since it passed into other hands, but every day when I pass its gates the grace of its former existence jogs my memory. One year recently, an exceptional winter frost seared the pomegranate hedge which borders the road into a tangle of apparently lifeless twigs, and I felt as if an old friend had been unfairly treated by nature. Later it recovered, and with it our good spirits as we pass that corner of Les Calans, with the bearded shepherd, like a biblical wayfarer, sometimes waving us on as we pass him with his flock.

With the move to Tarascon Bobbie and Yves were faced with an entirely different project, for their tall, eighteenth-century house, a building of a certain grandeur in the rue de l'Amoureux, has a courtyard severely limited in space, where the very high walls rob it of a great deal of sunlight. To enjoy more spring and autumn sun, small terraces were made at higher levels over outbuildings, and from one of them a system of falling water was devised which drops finally into a lily pond at ground level, its sound inducing an atmosphere of Buddhist serenity. The house and yard had been derelict for years, so rich alluvial soil from the banks of the Rhône had been brought in. The task of making a garden here was the antithesis of that in the Alpilles, where we can start near the house and spread gradually further into the wild, for here the only extension possible was vertically up the towering walls.

At the rue de l'Amoureux, a large proportion of the planting was transported in the boot of my car from Hilliers of Winchester. The most rigorous selection of plants had been mandatory since every inch of ground was valuable, every corner designed to exploit the vertical spaces. The rival merits of different varieties (all those unobtainable in Provence) had been mulled over with exquisite nicety and not a little indecision, but finally the choice was made. From England came the *Magnolia grandiflora* 'Exmouth', chosen for its promise of flower before too many years have passed. From its two-foot-high twiggy beginnings, within three years it produced its first luscious flower, and it is now in coolly opulent bloom, exotically enhanced by an underplanting of a spotted ligularia. The *Hibiscus syriacus* 'Diana' is now superb in its puckered purity, a 'Wedding Day' rose brought for the middle terrace now reaches to the heavens, while the delicate *Clematis macropetala* 'Markham's Pink' was chosen to enhance the deep blue spires of the *Echium candicans* (syn. *fastuosum*) of Riviera origin. Also on the middle terrace the 'Nevada' rose mixes with white jasmine, and a 'Marguerite Hilling' (both roses also brought from England) was chosen to spill over the edge. I was the happy recipient from this load of a *Carpenteria californica* which, it was discovered, would have claimed too great a space.

The walls were quickly clothed in green, and even non-climbers seem to romp upwards for the green-fingered Bobbie, among them white geraniums and a local rose. Then, as well as the irrepressible 'Bobbie James', resembling the frills of a Victorian wedding dress, there is a 'Mermaid' perpetually in bloom, and over a recessed archway hangs the long fringed curtain of a *Wisteria floribunda* next to a pale-faced clematis. On a darker wall a *Hydrangea petiolaris*, underplanted with *Iris japonica*, fuchsia and herbaceous paeony, forms a shady corner of the dell. Below the 'Mermaid', a deep blue ceanothus surrounds a window, while for many seasons a *Cobaea scandens* eccentrically decided to survive through the winters, entirely covering the tallest wall of all.

At ground level there are paving stones of *pierre de Fontvieille*, their interstices planted with creeping alpines, mertensias, and campanulas of various heights, from the diminutive *C. portenschlagiana* to *C. pyramidalis* and *C. persicifolia*. Yet more roses, 'Jacques Cartier' and 'Ballerina', fill corners by the lily pool which echoes to the sound of water trickling from the pool on the higher terrace . The exotic aspects include not only the ligularias and echiums but also a fecund palm brought from Italy, a *Yucca gloriosa* and the arums surrounding the floating water lilies.

The enviable areas of wall covered in clambering and cascading climbers now give the garden the character almost of a dell in some luxuriant corner of a forest. Having arrived from the blazing dusty street and passed through the cool, darkened house, to come into this garden, momentarily blinded by the sudden sunlight, is to marvel at the sense of a nearly tropical plenitude. This is, however, achieved using plants predominantly from temperate climates, with only a few well-chosen exotics.

In his role as director of cultural events for the town of Tarascon, Yves enjoyed a most successful collaboration with the director of gardening and keeper of the municipal greenhouses, Georges Grillet, a smiling bearded man now in his late fifties yet strikingly youthful in appearance and outlook, who has worked here since he was a lad of 20. But it was with the arrival of Yves in the early eighties that the two men initiated a whole new style in public gardening which so enhances the beautiful old stone of the city. Their colours are glowing not garish, the borders of the little garden near the Château du Roy René are fresh and natural, the window boxes of public buildings with their lacy pink pelargoniums have a delicate airiness which saves the grey stone from any hint of the sombre oppressiveness which it frequently has in similar towns in the Languedoc. Small wonder that for the beauty and originality of its gardens Tarascon so often receives top

Monsieur Grillet and Yves Coutarel at the 1998 Floralies

The garden at Tarascon, created out of a heap of rubble, with the roses 'Wedding Day' (top) and 'Marguerite Hilling' (bottom)

prize in national or regional contests. At less public venues, however, Georges provides a succession of displays for special occasions. On my last visit I found him organizing, in a single morning, the temporary adornment of the Gendarmerie, the Lycée, the Mairie, and a little museum for their various celebration parties. He has become an encouraging friend to many gardening enthusiasts in the region and we all enjoy visiting his serres on the 'open days'. While we marvel at the range of his achievements, he is generous with his expertise and one always leaves brimming with adventurous ideas and renewed optimism. He simply will not allow one to be downhearted, and on hearing of a failure with a certain plant will immediately counter with 'Have you thought of trying it this way?' or he will propose another more amenable member of the same species. Those of our neighbours who have greenhouses have particular reason to be inspired by the achievements of Georges.

At the Floralies, the annual flower show in May, he mounts a spectacular exhibition of exotics in the Château du Roy René in Tarascon. The great entrance hall and its noble staircase are festooned with huge begonias, daturas, eupatorias. We were all astonished when we first saw the immense height of *Begonia coccinea* 'Speciosa', the blooms luxuriant overhead on their black canes which resemble giant bamboos. The many other such varieties of begonia (*B. luxurians, odorata, ulmifolia,* x *corallina*) thrusting upwards contrast with the opulent hanging bells of datura (*Brugmansia sanguinea, B.* x *candida* 'Grand Marnier', 'Alba' and 'Alba Rosea'). Each year it is a regal display which clearly would have delighted 'le bon Roi René', the fifteenth-century owner of the château who, among his many talents, was both poet and horticulturalist, living at a time when such developments as now occur in the range of cultivars would have been unimaginable. This remarkable King of Provence, René d'Anjou, was an enthusiast for roses, the Centifolias, Albas, and Damasks which had been brought from the Eastern Mediterranean by the Crusaders returning to Aigues-Mortes on the Camargue. He had himself travelled in northern Italy, admiring the new style of the Renaissance, and had brought from Venice the sculptor Francesco Laurano to fashion a tomb in the nearby church of Sainte-Marthe. He and his queen, 'La Reine Jeanne', are much-loved figures in Provençal history, and particularly in the town of Tarascon.

In the mid-eighties, Yves discovered in the basement of the Hôpital de Saint-Nicolas, tucked away in dusty packing cases, a set of seventeenth-century apothecary jars. As municipal cultural attaché he persuaded the town council to enter a long loan agreement with the *Département des Monuments Historiques*, which is responsible for the Château du Roy René. He then arranged the 207 pieces with their marble tables in an impressive display in a wing of the castle. Though smaller, it is a collection comparable to that in the Hospice de Beaune, and gives delight to all our guests who explore Tarascon. What more natural than that Yves's thoughts should then move to the herbs which would have flourished and been used later to fill those beautiful *faïence de Montpellier* jars? He conceived of making, on the grassy terrace outside the chamber in which the jars were displayed, an

Monsieur Grillet's giant begonias (top) and the hôtel particulier *in which his exhibition was staged for the 1998 Floralies*

apothecary garden such as would have existed in the time of the Roi René. I well remember the winter of 1986–7, when we all became fascinated by Yves's researches into the medicinal herbals of those times, by his finding illustrations of the form of such gardens in Les *Très Riches Heures du Duc de Berry*, and by his discovery of the pattern of fountains and trellises in similar texts of the period, as well as a beautiful design for an octagonal fountain in a medieval illustration. There was to be a symmetry of forty plots, each devoted to a single variety of herb – I remember having pleaded for a nutmeg tree as it is mentioned in Chaucer, 'And note muge to put in ale'. Yves's herbarium was one of the most enjoyable preoccupations of that winter; we all began to search in books for appropriate herbs, and in nurseries for our own plantings, while the gardening neighbours loved gleaning ideas that derived from Yves's meticulous sense of history. Alas, whoever in the *Département des Monuments Historiques* was responsible for putting the plan into action had much less historical sense, so that the confusion of anachronistic elements that were introduced made us sad that such a good idea had not been carried through in the way it had been conceived. But the original plans still exist, so we hope they will be realized at some equally happy and appropriate site. The charming Pavillon de la Reine Jeanne in the Vallée des Baux springs to mind, for undoubtedly the good Roi René would find this herb garden worthy of his queen.

Some ten years after we had settled in Provence we heard with great pleasure that our friend Roderick (Rory) Cameron had bought and was restoring a derelict farmhouse in the Vaucluse, between Ménerbes and Les Baumettes. Many years earlier we had often stayed as his guests at La Fiorentina on the Saint-Hospice promontory of Saint-Jean-Cap-Ferrat. There in 1945, just after the war's end, he had created for his mother, Lady Kenmare, a superb garden in a spacious, formal style suited to the grand Palladian proportions of the house.

The site of La Fiorentina was majestic. It overlooked the wide expanse of the Beaulieu Bay, dotted with scudding sailboats and bound by the huge mountain range of the French and Italian Alpes Maritimes, the whole coastline giving an atmosphere of regal festivity. Indeed, for its greatest impact this view depends upon the blazing Riviera sun, for when the sky is overcast it has the cheerless air of a ballroom in dust sheets. Rory had designed the garden to introduce and enhance this panorama, with a flight of wide, shallow, grassy steps, flanked by Falconet sphinxes, descending to the sea. On either side were long grassed terraces extending laterally between high, sweetly scented hedges of *Pittosporum tobira*. The line of steps was bordered on each side by the elegant, tall needle forms of Italian cypress underplanted with echiums. Nothing could have had more serene splendour.

A little later he had transformed the smaller garden of La Fiorentina's eighteenth-century dower house, Le Clos, with terraces of secret gardens, formal, box-edged parterres, mandarin and lemon trees, making a virtue of the stylized miniature in frivolous contrast to the severe spaciousness of La Fiorentina itself. Still later he had bought and re-created an old Georgian rectory in County Donegal, where he was a neighbour of our mutual friend Henry McIlhenny, whose garden at Glenveagh Castle is among the very great. Knowing well and admiring Rory's previous creations, each keenly yet quietly attuned to the spirit of the place, we felt welcoming anticipation at the news of his arrival in our region.

The Vaucluse site was in stark contrast to those of La Fiorentina and Le Clos. The countryside of the Luberon valley is of wild, *maquis*-clad hills surrounded by simple agriculture of vines and cherry orchards. Already at only one northerly remove from the valley of the Alpilles, it is too cold for the extensive cultivation of olives. Facing south to the Montagne du Luberon, but some five miles away from it, Les Quatres Sources (as he named his new domain) commanded the view of the mountain's long, low outline, distance giving it a smoothness which belies its ponderous and rugged nature as it appears towering gloomily above Ménerbes, when one stands in that little hill town. From Rory's terrace, seen from behind the slender trunks of foreground Chinese mulberries, the Luberon gave one a sense of unending tranquillity. Its veiled contour seemed a deeper southern echo of the English chalk downland's purity of line, which like a calm maritime view evokes in one a Keatsian sentiment:

'Oh, ye who have your eyeballs vexed and tired,
Feast them upon the wideness of the sea – or of the Downs'

The farmhouse, soon to be extended by the addition of a large drawing room wing, stood on a steep slope covered by a tangle of neglected holm oak, other indigenous shrubs and dense undergrowth. The land seemed irredeemably scruffy, confused, and the most unlikely choice for a man of Rory's fastidious temperament, with his love of orderly charm. During the rebuilding, when he and his friend Gilbert Occelli camped out in a few tiny rooms of the farmhouse, we arrived one day on a neighbourly visit to find them engaged in the gargantuan task of cleaning the trunks of the holm oaks. Each tree was released from its tangle of undergrowth and lower boughs, and then its grey, knobbly trunk, like a gnarled form of birch, ascended clean and free to a high parasol of foliage. This stretch of maquis, cleared to ground level, was transformed into long, winding walks thus canopied by the holm oaks, the dappled light and shade playing upon the lichen and silver-grey trunks. Paths followed the dry-stone walls they had made to terrace the slope, and the planting was delicate and episodic.

It was a naturalistic, woodland garden, carpeted in spring by drifts of blue or white

*The Luberon from Rory's terrace, with
Ménerbes under rain clouds in the distance*

Anemone blanda fluttering in the breeze, and by innumerable clumps of bulbs brought from far-off climes (Turkey, Persia, and the Balkans), but looking as if they had lived there always. In the glinting light of spring the whole vista had the quietly scintillating air of a Seurat. Yet within this natural copse each grouping of shrubs provided a fresh, gentle diversion from the preceding one as we wandered down the long, serpentine path to the little newly planted orchard below, where in single file we could mount the steep, rough-hewn stairway through the low shrubs back to the house. At focal points on this descending walk there were romantic statues, urns and obelisks, weathered memorials to friends or to family .

Only surrounding the house did Rory allow himself, perhaps nostalgically, a more formal design. Near the entrance a silver border of monumental cardoons, 'Lochinch' buddleias, white roses, tapering down to a foreground of ballotas, ragworts and grey-leaved rock roses, seemed a tenuous evocation of his Irish rectory, and served as a prelude to the dignity of the house. Then, in a corner by the house wall, there was a small, rectangular box-edged parterre with topiary pyramids, and crammed with blue pansies, which struck friends who had known such patterns at Le Clos as an autobiographical aside, like a throwaway line in conversation, recalling with pleasure but no regrets the charm of a previous existence.

The sunny terrace fronting the new drawing room was planted in a design of deep greens and pale greys, consisting only in herbs of the locality – creeping rosemaries, clipped mounds of lavender and santolina, and clumps of sage and thyme. This sensitive pattern of *garrigue* colours served as an intermediary in the transition from the poised, treasure filled interior to the wild Luberon view, seen above the dark-foliaged treetops of the steep slopes below. In a corner of the terrace at ground level the giant splayed-out fingers of *Trachycarpus fortunei* palm leaves made an exotic foil to this indigenous planting.

In our renewed friendship with Rory, Stephen and I found a kindred spirit in the endless adventure of reconciling English plantsmanship with Mediterranean conditions. It was like a long-running game, played sometimes by telephone but often on visits to and fro. Rory was quick to notice each new introduction, warm in either commendation or commiseration, and imperturbably playful about the whole enterprise. On a visit to Saint-Jérôme he would instantly spot a new piece in the game, like a wild card in poker. 'Oh, you've found a so-and-so,' he would say. 'How clever of you! Well, good luck, because it's not as easy in the south as one hopes, but it will be lovely JUST THERE. Bravo!' Although his climate was noticeably harsher than ours, we were planting from the same range of subjects and could equally claim the mistral as perennial cause for any failures. There would be expeditions to neighbouring *départements* to see how plants might 'do' in ours.

The *bambouserie* near Alès, on the edge of the Cévennes, with its great range and variety of bamboos, caused us some excitement, though alas, its sheltered watery micro-climate was in sharp contrast to our exposed and arid sites. Its great forest clumps of the black-stemmed giants and the clearings with East Asian huts, exotic shrubs and channels

Rory Cameron at Les Quatres Sources

The long allée *leading with serpentine turns down the hillside*

of burbling water we found entrancing. But among the great collection there were species which we thought might follow the example of the naturalized *cannes de Provence* and make their home with us. On the homeward journeys from these forays the conjectural conversations would tend to go over the top, 'Imaginary plant associations' being the game played on these occasions.

Rory had a great influence on some local nurserymen, hitherto resistant to any weaning from their long-standing '*jardin-publique*' ideas. On an impulse visit to the *pépiniériste*, one might easily catch sight of his tall figure, gently ambling round the trees and shrubs like a tender-hearted giraffe, in persuasive conversation with the proprietor. Then, sure enough, in due course several varieties new to the region

Standing on Rory's staircase: Stephen, Rory, myself, Iris and Rodrigo

A corner of the terracing at Les Quatres Sources

would make their appearance. To his friends he would, in a reflective, diffident manner, make suggestions that were quite startling. Anne Cox Chambers once discovered him at her house making some quite radical rearrangement. 'Awfully cheeky of me to try this,' he said as she approached. She laughed. 'I wouldn't permit it in anyone else – but go right ahead!' was her answer.

It is only a very few years since Anne Cox Chambers arrived in the Alpilles, searching for a home in the French-speaking corner of Europe she had come to love during her time as United States Ambassador to Belgium. Seeking simplicity, for she was anti-château minded, she was at once captivated by the dramatic contours of the Alpilles and their unpretentious farms. On her first visit, she found Le Petit Fontanille, an old farmhouse surrounded by a large *terrain* of *maquis* hidden in the mountain behind the Romanesque chapel of Saint-Gabriel. Within a short time she had created one of the most remarkable gardens of the South of France, extended year by year as she 'spreads her conquests further', taming the tangled growth which had obscured the ancient Roman site, with its ruined aqueduct. The pervasive calm and antiquity of the site is restored and cherished within the boundaries of this garden of memorable plantings and design.

An early memory which surfaces as I now contemplate this perfectly composed garden, is of the slight figure of Anne, wrapped in her dark green loden, wandering alone through the wooded hillside, pausing to brood upon every vista. She knows every inch, envisages every projected contour and reflects long before taking each new decision. She is always generous in her praise of her early mentors, for many have enjoyed contributing ideas now absorbed into a finely orchestrated whole; nevertheless, a single spirit has created the harmony within which these diversities flourish.

Her first adviser, Peter Coats, was less than extravagant in his appreciation of the original site, with its decrepit, deeply rutted farmyard where carts were assembled in front of the traditional *mas*. After a long, silent exploration of the entire site extending to the ridge, he returned with the verdict, 'Well, it's no Versailles, and you can't make it one, but you have some beautiful trees.' Though all else would have to be imagined and created, the trees included gleditsia, sophora, acacia, and micocouliers before the house, as well as a neglected *allée* unevenly planted with cypress leading to the *maquis*-clad ridge but ending apparently nowhere. It was this unkempt vista lacking a focal point which had originally fired her imagination with a compelling urge to create a garden.

The barren stretch before the house was quickly transformed into a spacious lawn where the elegant old trees now cast long traceries of shadows. The barnyard became a stone-paved terrace set with large terracotta pots of sweet geranium and jasmine. The *allée* was restored with shallow, grassy steps between the tapered forms of Italian cypress which chime with the obelisk she eventually found and placed in the woods beyond. Then they made another ascending walk, serpentine and shadowy with subtly-coloured foliage, silvery eucalyptus and oleaster (*Elaeagnus angustifolia*, and known locally as 'Olivier de Bohème') making phantom presences above the darker foliage of purple berberis, *Prunus pissardii*, and the rich blue of evergreen ceanothus. The pale trunks of lagerstroemia trees like twisted skeins of beige silk, the white of banksiae roses and foxgloves, the pale green of a contorted willow, all contribute to the cool mystery of this winding, shady path, to which one is irresistibly drawn from the heat of midday sun.

The foreground included a large old palm; its scraggy trunk was soon obscured behind a lush underplanting of choisya, yucca, *Fatsia japonica*, and the large rounded leaves of *Ligularia veitchiana*. As one arrives by the broad stone staircase from the cobbled yard below, one passes a box-edged parterre alight with pale blue violas, a small signature left by Rory Cameron evoking our affectionate memories of his earlier creations and of the tireless, plant-finding expeditions we all enjoyed in his company.

Since those early days, each garden within a garden newly achieved at Le Petit Fontanille has a pleasing self-sufficiency, yet one is drawn to the next terrace or bend in the path which discloses a fresh variation or episode. The formality surrounding the house alternates with informal borders, which in turn lead to a merging with nature at the periphery. In the lee of the cypress *allée* stands a small formal garden leading to a simple grotto. One bitter winter's day I came upon Rosemary Verey contemplating some overgrown olives in this elegant plot, somehow too ragged for the geometric perfection of their setting. They needed to make more of a statement, she thought. Then, with the air

of a sudden inspiration, she said that the shapes needed were those of 'giant lollipops'. No sooner said than, with Anne's welcoming assent, she was up on a tall *chevalet* in her warm quilted jacket and mittens, clipping away and transforming not only the giant heads of the trees, but also the entire character of this small garden.

We were all captivated by Rosemary, with her throwaway manner of making original, even startling, suggestions, and her supremely erudite and meticulous sense of garden history concealed behind a kind of quiet nonchalance. Above all, she was unfailingly kind, and although she must at times have found one's ignorance amusing, her encouraging pleasure at one's tentative ideas kindled enthusiasm. We all recognized her as not only an inspired gardener, but also a born teacher with the added virtue of 'one-downmanship'.

More recently, Le Petit Fontanille has seen the creation of a spacious, formal rose garden with stone urns and a plashing fountain. But the originality lies in the steep bank which surrounds this garden, planted almost entirely in soft tones of pink and blue, white and grey. Its informality and abundance make the ideal foil and frame to the strict geometry of the rose-filled parterre, and at the same time the ideal transition to the grassy olive orchard and the dark green woods above. Then there is a scented herb-filled allée, in which it is impossible to resist pinching or plucking tiny leaves as one strolls towards an orangery, with its exotic shrubs in large terracotta pots and its charming grotto.

The whole *domaine* rests enclosed within a wide declivity of the mountain, surrounded by pinewoods and approached by way of its vineyards. To the west, however, there is an open view stretching beyond the Rhône, which it is particularly restful to contemplate at sunset from a terrace overlooking a lavender field and, beyond that, the herb and cutting gardens. A few cypresses grouped at the extremity of this garden vista enhance the wide, horizontal lines of the distant view. This view, one of the many subtleties of naturalistic design as one turns away from the formal gardens, avoids both the French and the Italian conventions of planting cypress; indeed, one is quite unaware that the picture has been composed, for the trees might well be survivors from antiquity.

It often happens that my autumn visit to Saint-Jérôme with friends who help me with my olive harvest coincides with a house party of gardening friends at Le Petit Fontanille, engaged on some new planting venture. Every evening as we arrive from a hard day's olive picking, we stroll out to see the gardeners' progress, from bare earth and bulldozers to rich composting, then the placing of trees, a skeletal design soon clothed with new, as yet skimpy, shrubs. Then comes the day when kneelers and trowels supersede the heavy tools

Roses 'White Meidiland' and 'Raubritter' in the impressive steep bank, and Rory Cameron's box-edged parterre alight with violas at Le Petit Fontanille

and one can scarcely believe the speed with which a whole new creation has come into being. After dark, the garrulous gathering as we assemble for dinner, fizzing with gardeners' gossip, is pervaded by a cheerful sense of achievement.

What emerges after some years of the pleasures of these gardening friendships, is how very much we have learned from each other, as well as from our talented guests, and how fond we become of each others' *domaines*. If the elements or the soil behave badly, we feel our commiseration for each other, almost as we would if one of our children were to be passing through a difficult phase. If a new neighbour arrives in the Alpilles, looking forward to transforming a *terrain*, we feel a warm enthusiasm whilst slightly envying them the fun of starting from scratch. For notwithstanding the peculiarities of our climate, there seems to be no end to the fund of ideas generated between us. We seem to be both severally and mutually enticed into new inventiveness, into a wider vocabulary from which to compose, and into heady new imaginings. This November as I write, sitting far away in London, my thoughts are of Yves's plan to transform their courtyard into a muted mosaic of colours; of Anne's project of wilder woodland walks of flowering trees and bulbs beneath the pine canopy of the remote hillside; of my own plans for transforming the outer edge of the Meadow Garden to merge in more subtle tones with the olive orchard beyond, and for a carpet of creeping thyme on a small plateau of my pine-clad hillside.

Have we all by now gathered and distilled the wisdom needed for creating a garden of western Provence? Certainly we have come a long way, and so too have the prevailing ideas within our region. As our gardens have matured, a style has emerged which has in some ways profited from earlier, milder, gardens of the Côte d'Azur, so many of them made by Edwardian English or American fugitives from the north. In other ways we have learned from those well-known gardens of harsher northern climates. Yet our landscape, and the trees and flowers which naturally thrive within it, does tend towards endowing a distinct characteristic, which it is most enjoyable to foster, and which is perhaps becoming unique.

The Rose Garden in June

CHAPTER 9

Here and Now

Unlike painting or sculpture or buildings a garden grows.
Its appearance changes – plants mature, some in six weeks, some in six hundred
years. There are few gardens that can be left alone.

RUSSELL PAGE, 'THE EDUCATION OF A GARDENER', 1962

Nineteen ninety-five is to be remembered as the year of transmutation. I had been sadly unable to visit in the two previous years, and in the meantime the inevitable neglect had taken over. Though prepared to be philosophical, I was also resolved to welcome as a challenge the gaps and wayward usurping of them by weeds and seedlings, some already waist-high. It encouraged me, in a time of sadness, to think of fulfilling so many intentions which had hitherto been left in abeyance; perhaps it was even a heaven-sent opportunity to look at the scene as if I were a stranger, and to think of a future when my grandchildren might enjoy it in maturity.

Seeing the main vistas thus wrapped in confusion made me wonder if an artist deciding to paint over a canvas which he has rejected as not realizing his intentions, feels nevertheless haunted by his original idea. Or indeed, when reinterpreting a work of music after a long gap in a lifelong familiarity, to consider it with fresh mind and ears is both exhilarating and yet difficult entirely to achieve. As in gardening, the main structure is maturely there, and there is no temptation radically to refashion it, but very often details of nuance can transform one's understanding of the whole, giving it a fresh eloquence. I reflected that the rescue of my garden from its momentary decline could be just such an adventure in reviving a conception begun so many years ago.

That year had been notable for exceptional summer drought, followed by a deliciously mild October, and when I arrived in late November the shock of extremely unhappy wild cherries beset with disease was redeemed by the pleasure of seeing the rose garden enjoying a late surge of full bloom. Indeed 'La Follette' smothered the terrace wall with a most unusual second flush of its refreshing pink and, even more surprising, ceanothus and *Buddleja* x *weyeriana* were newly in leaf and flower amid the desolate confusion. Since the mild season allayed one's fear of early frost, these eccentricities of out-of-season exuberance were heartwarming.

With only a week to spare, even I was realist enough to know that one pair of hands could not begin the rescue operation. Then it was that my thoughtful friend Anne Chambers gave me a present most joyfully received – her team of three gardeners for a whole day. They swept in upon the scene of wilting neglect like a tornado, the handsome head gardener, Serge, directing his colleagues to the four corners, chopping down the diseased trees, rooting out the dying lavender and berberis, spraying viburnums and fruit trees, tidying and weeding, and building a huge pile of debris in the olive orchard to await the permissible season for a bonfire.

Having by now amassed some Mediterranean know-how, one could see at once the scope for new introductions within the main idea, and one could review with a fresh pair of eyes the changes in proportions and shapes which had occurred through the maturing of shrubs at different tempos over the years, and through a few inevitable losses. Moreover, it was possible to revive earlier ideas in the light of newly available varieties and to envisage the character of the whole garden twenty years hence. This must come somewhat after my time, and it is a happy thought that it might flourish in maturity under the incandescent light of Provence when, I hope, my great-grandchildren will enjoy it, with perhaps a carefree lack of curiosity as to its history.

There had been a month during *les grandes chaleurs* when plans had misfired. In our absence no watering at all had taken place in July, so it was instructive to see which shrubs had succumbed, which had valiantly held on to life. All teucrium, buddleias, cistus, lilac, cytisus, arbutus, santolinas, sages and most but not all berberis were quite unperturbed. And of course those plants described locally as *increvable* had burgeoned or encroached, hypericum, choisya, and iris crying out to be divided and replanted. Some ceanothus, kolkwitzia, paeonies and climbing roses looked less than flourishing but had somewhat revived in the September rains. Quite a well-established *Colutea arborescens* had entirely given up the struggle, and a fairly new *Malus* 'Red Sentinel' was less than happy. After Serge and his rather jolly team had departed there remained a welter of more modest weeds still to be trowelled away, and some had so far invaded and tangled with the rosemary hedge that it was better to uproot and start again. But the new vistas revealed by some yawning gaps were inspiring, and as I reviewed the garden site by site, I was pleasantly surprised by a feeling of optimism.

The plants on the house wall had all done tolerably well, the imported 'Madame Alfred Carrière', 'Paul's Lemon Pillar' and 'Bobbie James' had all grown appreciably and are clearly suited to Mediterranean life. The native wisteria and campsis had celebrated their silver jubilee in style, the perennial morning glory had rampaged, the winter jasmine was a healthy but unruly tangle, and the oleanders had grown tall and very bushy. Only a 'Climbing Lady Hillingdon' rose had faded away, and I was sorry to lose her, but decided

The Pink Border and Maquis Garden

View from the east terrace with the mushroom form of horizontal juniper

that her lively yellow had rather disturbed the gentle rosy colour of that corner of the terrace, whereas 'Paul's' pale lemon has an enhancing effect.

The garden in front of the west terrace wall and around the steps to the Lilac Walk now presents more of a design challenge. Here, the long-loved favourites go happily on and live well together, though they were interspersed with a rather meaningless array. The favourites include a *Ribes speciosum* which had been brought from England after I had seen the magnificent specimen growing high on a wall in the Oxford Botanic Garden, though at Saint-Jérôme its growth has been remarkably slow. Its slim fuchsia-ish blooms associate well with its neighbouring climbing 'Hermosa' (the China rose brought from the old Sunningdale Nursery), which has more charmingly tight-packed blooms than some I have seen elsewhere. Indeed, their almost rosette form resembles the 'Schneezwerg' roses which used to front it at the foot of the wall, until falling casualty to the recent drought. 'La Follette' dominates the extent of this wall, with a white *Abutilon vitifolium*, a lemon verbena, and a floriferous 'Duchess of Marlborough' tree paeony in the foreground. These mature subjects are treasured. But as it then stood, having arisen largely by accident in early days, the pink-and-white candy-coloured theme was less sensitive than one would have wished. A dwarf hedge of deep violet 'Hidcote' lavender encloses this border, adding to the strong hues and to the problem of introducing more harmony to the whole.

It was evident that very pale colours and feathery foliage simply made the strong colours of the old-timers more dominating, while themselves losing character, becoming merely wishy-washy. So I flirted with several ideas before coming to the decision to move out the pale caryopteris and an elderly common sage, in order to move in rather stronger, less cloudy forms. I finally decided on a 'Ballerina' rose as a pink-and-white link to the white abutilon, a 'Perle d'Azur' clematis for late bloom on the wall, and the stronger, bronze-violet tones of *Salvia nemorosa* to help the Hidcote lavender join in the harmony. Glossy foliage would help, with the large periwinkle for spring bloom. The craving for scent which seizes one in springtime is satisfied by blood-red wallflowers which coincide with the bronzy new foliage of 'La Follette', and in winter that sheltered corner of the terrace will be pervaded by the perfume of a newly planted *Chimonanthus praecox*. One impulse after-thought that I was unable to resist when packing the car in London for a subsequent spring visit was a pure white flowering currant which was agreeably squeezed into the terrace scheme. Perhaps to the English imagination this blend of contrasts might seem a little too strong, or even a jumble, but under the beating sun of a Provençal summer the

The recently installed Lutyens bench in the Rose Garden surrounded by the China rose 'Perle d'Or' and the pomegranate hedge behind, past its flowering

Steps leading down to the Lilac Walk with
Carpenteria californica *on the left and*
'Canary Bird' rose (detail) on the right

colours merge together more gently, and the terrace-wall garden, unrelieved by shade, is the place for it. 'Well', I thought, 'we shall see how these innovations mature.'

Descending the stairs into the Lilac Walk, passing beyond the sunny yellow of 'Canary Bird' and *hugonis* roses which overhang the steps, all is shady and cool as summer unfolds; so for this boon one must tolerate its moments of gloom at the winter solstice when few of the sun's rays can penetrate. It has grown into a lofty, narrow corridor of deep-green cypresses, against which the white blooms of flowering shrubs seem like the glow of tapers in a darkened church. These high proportions of maturity seem to impel one towards the destination where the broader square of David's Mycenaean pot invites one to pause and rest. However, the helleborus varieties in the Lilac Walk seem to enjoy life in the shadows, and in early spring the pale primroses and the delicate violets are more than contented under the towering *Magnolia grandiflora*. The huge photinia is in bloom very early, and the 'Bridal Wreath' spiraeas are quite spectacular in this somewhat subdued light. In April the lilacs and white iris give a great lift to the solemnity of the scene. The only large shrub to have somewhat lost its élan with the increasing shade is the pure-white tree paeony 'Mrs William Kelway', and any attempt to move her is not to be contemplated. The later-flowering abelia and *Hibiscus syriacus* do very well in a rather more fortunate position,

The Lilac Walk

where shafts of light filter through some narrow gaps between the cypresses, while the white oleanders and buddleias which alternate regularly with the lilacs on the north side are now profuse in high summer. A surprising success, although now in comparative shadow, is the floriferous *Carpenteria californica*. At that season some sunlight from directly overhead at midday reduces the air of mystery, at its best in the hours around dawn or dusk. But the main problem continues to be that of finding subjects for a shade-loving underplanting of the wide, episodic south border.

Since in Provence it is essential to protect campanulas from being burnt by the sun, I am hoping for success with *C. alliariifolia* and *C. carpatica* in this position. The white foxgloves enjoy their corner, and white valerian mingling with the Walter Ingwersen form of *Geranium renardii* are equally happy. Although *Lilium henryi* enjoys the shade, our very limey soil favours but few lilies, and the intention is to grow the white martagons in large pots to place by the stone seats. Curiously enough, there has been no great success with hostas, which would be an obvious choice for this walk, but in spite of the shade, the ground can become very dry in summer, even though regularly watered, so they have been replaced by *Bergenia* 'Silberlicht' with a white thalictrum for later bloom. A group of yuccas at the end of the walk gives interest late in the season, their cumbersome trunks having been screened by *Fatsia japonica*, although that, alas, foundered in the last season, and will take time to replace to any great height.

In general, a great part of one's ingenuity in Mediterranean gardens must be directed to prolonging the colour into the long weeks of dry heat in high summer. In western Provence, which is far from frost-free, many of the Côte d'Azur plants – for instance echiums, bougainvilleas, and of course orange and lemon trees – need greenhouse protection in winter, and are out of the question for those without such facilities. Thus for partially absentee gardeners oleanders, recurrent roses and annuals are very often the main standbys for colour in high summer, and it needs a little care to site them harmoniously.

This necessity had particularly concerned us in the Barberry Walk, where colours on the bronze and pale yellow side of the spectrum are simple to accommodate in spring, yet later in the season can be less easy to sustain. In addition, the soil had also been troublesome, bordering as it does an area of very poor marl. At this north-west corner of the garden the mistral is at its most ferocious and the windbreak most difficult to establish, so that the more robust shrubs within the walk have proved invaluable. These include the berberis, arbutus, and *Cotinus coggygria*, forming a sheltered corner screened from the Rose Garden by the pomegranate hedge behind them. There have been surprising successes within their shelter, notably an abutilon with hanging bell-like flowers of a rich, soft red almost like crushed strawberries. Since I had found it in the market at Arles, there is little clue to its exact identity, though it most closely resembles 'Ashford Red'.

Early in the season there are irises of wonderfully exotic hue, a preference for selfs, rather than contrasts between standards and falls, having been the only guiding principle within

The Barberry Walk: Looking north (above), with orange mimulus in the left foreground; the southern end (opposite) with the apricot-toned medicago, the warm grey dorycniums, a 'Graham Thomas' rose and Euphorbia mellifera *in the foreground; the toffee-coloured 'Tarn Hows' iris (below)*

'Buff Beauty' rose in the Grey Walk

'Golden Wings' rose (far left) in the Lilac Walk; philadelphus (top) and an old blush China rose (bottom) in the Rose Garden

this bronzy colour range. They include the toffee-coloured 'Tarn Hows' and others ranging from burgundy red to a golden apricot, and yet another of the palest primrose yellow. As time has gone by, I have found that the pale yellow tones, as in the single pale yellow oleanders and the 'Golden Wings' rose, are essential in introducing a certain airiness into what had promised to become a heavy preponderance of scarlets and crimsons. In summer a similar lightening of the spectrum is provided by the pale apricot tones of hemerocallis and a beautiful shrubby mimulus (*M. aurantiacus*) which blooms for many months. These tones are faintly echoed by the 'Mrs Oakley Fisher' roses. We found that there could too easily be a dominance of sword-like foliage with the day lilies, crocosmias, iris and knifophias, and this is softened by a group of *Salvia grahamii* and another of broom, with a flourishing clump of phlomis in the background. Alas, the elegant *Melianthus major* was burnt by a particularly bitter mistral, and though it was moved into the shelter of the Rose Garden, it was reluctant to revive to its former abundance. The desire for some purple foliage in perennials was disappointed in *Heuchera* 'Palace Purple', which started well in each early spring but in that corner it also soon became burnt by the wind; however, *Euphorbia amygdaloides* 'Purpurea' is more robust, enjoyably rich in tone and bushy in form. In general, euphorbias enjoy Provençal conditions; indeed, there are varieties of *E. characias* and *E. polychroma* growing wild throughout the Alpilles. But at Saint-Jérôme we regret failures with *E. griffithii* 'Fireglow' – nor, I remember, did it survive at Les Quatre Sources in the Vaucluse. It is evident that Asian varieties of euphorbia are less happy in Provence than those descended from the European species. However, we must be grateful for the success of *E. mellifera*, *E. robbiae*, and of course, *E. myrsinites* in various corners of the garden.

Of the trees planted in the Barberry Walk an *Acer platanoides* has developed especially well, its blossom before the leaves unfold having a strange beauty. On the other hand, that slow-grower, *Acer griseum*, whilst always pleasing with its cinnamon-ish peeling bark and translucent, brilliant autumn leaves, has made so little growth in height and span that I suspect it is over buried limestone rock. This is a condition we have discovered to be the case in some other corners of our land, where even a single olive tree in a row can appear unaccountably stunted, until one notices that it is on a line continuing a more distant rocky outcrop. There are two other slender trees behind the shrubs in this walk which are also slow in growth though charming in form, a red lagerstroemia and a *Rhus typhina*, both

Day lily (above), callistemon (right),
and mimulus (centre) in the Barberry Walk,
and the Cytisus battandieri *in the Grey Walk*

providing warm colour in late summer. There are no great innovations of trees or shrubs needed in the Barberry Walk (although I would welcome yet more colourful autumn fruits since at that season the colours in this end of the garden give especial pleasure), and one is left with the comparatively lighthearted task of introducing more diversity of foliage and flower form amongst the perennials.

It sometimes surprises me that people express a conscientious objection to one colour in gardens, and that it often turns out to be yellow. But one cannot live in Van Gogh country and banish it from one's thoughts. However, in the confines of the garden it does need to be treated more delicately than in the wild, or in the large fields of oil-seed rape or of sunflowers which are fleetingly enjoyable as one drives past them. Except for the brilliant blooms of *Verbascum olympicum* on their woolly grey spires, and a touch in the Austrian copper briar rose, the softer, paler yellows in the Barberry borders are more pleasing. But at the southern end of the walk it seemed the place to introduce slightly stronger yellows, in transition towards the Grey Walk. They are gently mediated by a *Coronilla* 'Citrina', beyond which the sulphur rose (*R. hemisphaerica*) and the comparatively new 'Graham Thomas' have star quality, suitably surrounded by the warm grey dorycniums, and by achilleas the colour of oatmeal. One modern rose, 'Golden Days', a present for our golden wedding in 1991, has gone modestly on, tucked in its niche away from the main vista, although not yet quite living up to the panache of its neighbours. A shrub which thrives in this corner arouses my curiosity, as it is well known in our district as 'medicago', and has early apricot-toned blossom and foliage resembling that of coronilla. However, this name does not satisfy some English gardening friends, who tell me that to be a true medicago it would have to look like a clover bush. I await further knowledgeable verdicts, but whatever its name and lineage, I am devoted to its cheerful charm.

The main effect of maturing shrubs at the southern end of the Barberry Walk has been the loss of the wide vista towards the great slabs of sloping rock overhanging the lane which winds down to the valley below the house. It is now a rather more enclosed and less dramatic garden, and one's pleasure in that view is postponed until one reaches the Grey Walk. The new enthusiasm is for giving much more height to the vista seen from the Mycenaean corner by extending the planting to the higher level, choosing more wind-resistant shrubs, as well as reinforcing the hedge which must take the brunt of the gales.

Turning into the Grey Walk past a huge teucrium, the prospect is entirely Mediterranean, for little else will thrive in the great heat of a southern exposure with no shade. In early spring the pale mauve iris and the bushes of coronilla seem to take over, except for the heavy, blush-coloured blossoms of *Prunus* 'Okumiyako', which have their spectacular moment, and a foreground of white Roman osteospermum, *Convolvulus cneorum*, *Helianthemum* 'Wisley Primrose', cerastium and dwarf bulbs. There follows a quick succession of flowering; at the back of the border there are apple and quince blossom, a delicate pale mauve species lilac (probably a French form of *Syringa* x *persica*),

The acacia boule *in early Spring, set between the Rose Garden and the Grey Walk*

The Grey Walk and a 'Madame Hardy' rose

fremontodendron, then a row of *Buddleja alternifolia* and a bush of *Cytisus battandieri*, while further forward the large white cistus daily shed their petals like snowflakes and continue in sparkling bloom. The roses have a delectable moment with the 'Madame Hardy', and thereafter there is the soft apricot of 'Buff Beauty' and the rather more temperamental 'Apricot Nectar'. The cloudy blue-mauve tones are perpetuated by alliums, perovskias and large nepetas, while the romneyas often bloom at the same time as Mount Etna broom. After the coronillas have subsided into dull foliage they are covered with the rather starry *Clematis* 'Minuet'. There is nothing particularly original about this whole planting, but it has survived in quite a pleasing way, distinct in character and yet making a good transition between the western perimeter of the garden and the *maquis* planting which faces the house. It demands no radical rethink, but only a little accommodating of shrubs which have been obscured by the more robust growth of their neighbours. Apart from the day lilies, *Santolina rosmarinifolia* 'Primrose Gem' and the temperamental *Convolvulus sabatius* among the artemisias, there could be much more foreground colour in high summer, and I enjoy inviting suggestions from visitors, for when the factors of position and hue are taken into account it is not such an easy game to play, and the most experienced gardeners become intrigued. It is surprising that eryngiums have not exactly thrived in this border as yet, since other thistles such as echinops and the troublesome onopordums grow wild in our olive orchards.

Turning the eastern corner of the walk into the pink borders, the transition is helped by the pale coral colour of 'Doris' pinks below *Lavatera* 'Barnsley', and a 'Baroness Rothschild' rose of a particularly gentle disposition. However, once having arrived, one finds these borders unashamedly bright with *Cistus albidus* over a long season, sugar-pink paeonies, the spectacular 'Lord Selborne' tree paeony, and the clear vitality of 'Complicata', 'Scabrosa' and 'Marguerite Hilling' roses. The softening, more feathery character is contributed by kolkwitzia, tamarisk, a pale Persian lilac, and the 'Constance Spry' rose in front of the apple blossom screen. The blue of ceanothus and *Hibiscus syriacus* 'Blue Bird' and the cloudy white of gaura also contribute to a mild and mellowing effect upon the more brilliant pink. Looking down at it from the house or the terrace, there is no sense of blaze, but rather of a warm harmony. Late summer sees the deep pink of a lagerstroemia which has, at long last, matured and decided to bloom. Fortunately, for it can have a dangerous stridency, the surrounding colours soften its impact to a deep glow.

The Maquis Garden in front of the house has matured into a naturally undulating carpet of santolinas, sages, iris, symphoricarpos, horizontal junipers, and low-growing cistus with the taller tamarisk, *Buddleja globosa* and *B.* x *weyeriana* and wild cherries emerging gently from them. Here, our surprising and regretted losses in the untended year included a lespedeza, and it remains rather a quandary whether it should be replaced. Indigofera languished for a season but then revived. These had been brought from England and I have seen no other examples of them growing locally, so it is not easy to judge whether

*The Pink Border with Lord Selborne (above) in
the foreground, and the Pink Walk (right)*

Previous double page: Cistus *x* purpureus,
Teucrium fruticans *and berberis in the
Maquis Garden (right); Cistus, pale iris and
fremontodendron in the Grey Walk (left).
This cistus was bought locally as* C. laurifolius
*although the leaves don't quite match
this variety*

The kolkwitzia in the Pink Border

This page: The tamarisk and wild cherry in bloom

Following pages: View into the olive orchard with the wild cherry in bloom; and the Prunus 'Okumiyako' *in bloom*

173

they are less suited to local conditions. As they are not usually temperamental, my instinct is to try again, giving them more room to breathe and more tender loving care. Every year, at the appropriate moment, we shape the clumps of tamarisk and wild cherry to echo the lines of the hills beyond.

There remains the list of unfulfilled aspirations in my ages-old gardening book. This started all those years ago with *Catalpa bignonioides*, and there is now an appropriate place for one on the hillside just beyond the present confines of the garden, where the fresh pale green of its foliage would contrast with the deep tones of the pines behind it. But now, alas, it would run the hazard of the herd of goats which my neighbour regularly lets loose upon the land. A more attractive project, too long deferred, is to plant a paulownia where the land dips in the western corner of the olive orchard just beyond the retaining wall of the garden. Here we could look down upon it from the garden and the upper terrace, when its crown of mauve bloom would shine against the dark *pinède*, and be sheltered from the wind. The variety grown locally is *Paulownia tomentosa*, and although I have an affection for *Paulownia fargesii* which one sees flourishing at Exbury, I reluctantly own that it would be imprudent to expect such a large specimen to withstand our wind. It is a tantalizing consideration for most gardeners that there exist many more beautiful trees than can be accommodated in the confines of their gardens.

For anyone starting a Provençal garden at this time, there are trees of the locality which would be high on my list of suggestions, notably micocoulier, persimmon, and koelreuteria; and there is one I should dearly love to try, *Sophora tetraptera*, although I have seen only *Sophora japonica* in the vicinity. Micocoulier (*Celtis australis*) in this region grows into a huge yet graceful tree, which can live for centuries. With its elegant foliage it adorns many of the public gardens in the region, including that on the boulevard des Lices in Arles, which was painted by Van Gogh. Diospyros, the Chinese persimmon, known locally as the kaki tree, is resplendent in autumn and winter, with its tangerine-coloured fruit like tomatoes hanging on the bare branches. A friend used to decorate the Christmas dinner table with whole branches, seemingly growing out of the moss in which they were planted. When guests gasped at the beauty of the sight, she would murmur with a laugh, 'You are requested, with respect, not to eat the decorations!' *Koelreuteria paniculata*, the golden rain tree, rejoices in the hot dry summers of Provence where it too will grow into a tall spreading tree of some elegance, and with more yellow panicles of blossom than can be seen in our northern gardens. *Sophora japonica* 'Pendula' is very often seen in Provence forming a natural arbour with branches hanging to the ground. It can appear a little gloomy and formal. More preferable, given shelter from the wind, would be the glowing yellow

Iris border below the wild cherry trees

Vineyards just beyond the house

The edge of the Meadow Garden with native iris

trumpets of *Sophora tetraptera*, which luxuriates in the mild Gulf Stream gardens of the west of Ireland and, given shelter, could, I believe, be coaxed into doing well for us in Provence. Yet another of my aspirations is to banish all wistfulness about the unsuitability of our soil for deciduous magnolia, azaleas and so on, by making a virtue of viburnums. We have fared quite well with *Viburnum opulus*, *V. 'Anne Russell'*, *V. rhytidophyllum*, and of course the tough old *V. tinus*. But we are so well-disposed for all the *V. plicatum*, *V. x juddii*, *V. x burkwoodii*, that there seems no end of opportunity to enjoy the infinite variety of the species.

My new dream is to make a terrace in the angle below the steps which descend to the olive orchard, where the view is of the olives, *pinède* and rocks in the unspoilt valley, and where it would also be sheltered from the wind which sweeps across the garden. Here Providence has lent a hand since yet another crisis in the drains demanded a visit to the olive orchard by a team of plumbers and a powerful bulldozer, which also cleared a space

below the high retaining wall for the terrace-to-be. Needless to say, in true Provençal fashion the machine also cut the power line to the water cistern, so that the very day of my return in June was enlivened by colossal emergency and flurry over a seemingly unstoppable Niagara and its accompanying inundation. 'Hunt the electrician' seemed a losing game. However, in the evening, when all was finally remedied, the workmen, who had previously pulled long '*Que voulez-vous?*' faces, departed wreathed in smiles, with effusive good wishes for a peaceful holiday. At last I relaxed, exhausted, in the garden above, but musing contentedly, 'Here we are again: maximum aggro, at last resolved. Well, after all, Provence never changes.'

Nor, may I say, does my relationship with Provence. Although one is often charmed by other landscapes and envious of less harsh climates for gardening, it is difficult to imagine living elsewhere. Even to forsake our 'Val des Amants' for any other terrain in the region seems unthinkable. For this little rock-bound corner of the Alpilles and its garden continue to give back to us that happiness which has accrued year by year of our having rested and worked creatively whilst absorbing its beauty.

Natasha looking over the olive orchard from Granny's corner

Previous double page: Our orchard (top left) and the vineyards and olive orchard of local friends

A far corner of our fields

CHAPTER 10

Epilogue

Outside, the eternal star-tall mountains gleam
Where changeless changing past and future lock
Their fusing streams into one day of rock
Against whose day my days but shadows seem

STEPHEN SPENDER 'SPIRITUAL EXPLORATIONS', 1947

Provence is a Mecca for many immigrants from the bleak months of northern climates. But those devoted gardeners who come to the region are of two contrasting temperaments – the Paradise Seekers and the Paradise Dwellers.
The Seekers fall in love with the place of their dreams, preferably one in a state of spectacular neglect, and then fling themselves into its restoration with not a little fervour and fever. They are keen for speedy conversions and are often virtuosi at scintillating seasonal displays, but impatient with plants that may slowly go their own way. Naturally, the Seekers bask in the expressions of appreciation or astonishment which they receive for their transformations. They are a little ambivalent about newcomers, torn between a desire to help (particularly if the recent arrivals show a wish to emulate their triumphs), and a fear that their particular creation will no longer remain unique, notwithstanding that imitation is the most sincere form of flattery. For them, the journey and not the arrival matters, and the realization before long that they have achieved their envisaged perfection is somewhat of a calamity. They feel lost, or perhaps bored, when an immediate prospect of imposing an entire design no longer faces them, and like the dreaming Catherine in *Wuthering Heights* they feel restless in Paradise. Like her, they wish to be flung out upon a wild moorland, where they will awake, as she did, 'sobbing with joy' that they may set about another huge project of restoration. As their marriage to the beloved site of their creation begins to flag, they do not move very far, for their love of Provence is such that they find it difficult to fall in love with any other region; moreover, local fame is the spur. As in matrimony where successive partners often bear a striking resemblance to predecessors, it is seldom that the Paradise Seeker's new garden in a contrasting landscape is of a totally new and original character, for a recognizable signature is written large upon the land. More often it is a

185

performance which, in speed and panache, resembles that of the conjuror. One couple I knew went from an elegant *pavillon* to a huge castle with their personal flag at the masthead of the tower, and yet again to a third domain within the space of very few years.

The shining exception to this resolute stamping of identity on the landscape was Rory Cameron's Les Quatres Sources, which was in almost total contrast to his Irish garden or the earlier Riviera garden at La Fiorentina (though, of course Cap-Ferrat could not have been seen as *echt* Provençal). One cannot doubt, however, that he was not at heart a Seeker but, accepting changes of necessity in his circumstances, he overcame the sadness of departure, and then with time rose to the challenge of soaking his vision into an entirely new landscape and of sensitively moulding his garden within it. Tragically, he was granted too few years of dwelling in his ultimate Paradise.

Our friends and kindred spirits in the region have been Paradise Dwellers. Year by year their project is of pursuing or enhancing the original conception. If they are fortunate enough to push out the boundaries of their domains, then they are preoccupied with the relation of their new creation to that already in existence, much as a new baby is welcomed into the domestic circle. Even when their lives change in fundamental ways, children grown up and wandering away, or even in bereavement, they do not wish the further unhappiness of leaving their Paradise; indeed, they often lavish on it the loving care they are now unable, on a daily basis, to devote to the departed family. New projects tend not to be in the huge, radical style of the Paradise Seekers, for they do not wish to astonish their visitors, but only to enhance their memories of former times, and their enjoyment of continuity. And if the visitors are old friends, they arrive with the wish to rekindle the old affections; to see reflected in the garden the personalities of those who have created it; to refresh the love they have all shared for the landscape.

In Western Europe, the gradual confluence of taste in garden design which tends toward sensitivity to 'the genius of the place' has had a happy influence, in our region, upon the French as well as the recently settled foreign creators of gardens. When, in absence, I think of Saint-Jérôme, my mind's eye seems drawn to the etched and timeless skyline, then to float inwards over mounds of dark *maquis* and stretches of pale olives to the garden cradled on the edge of the hollow. In contrast, our most recently arrived neighbour, at perhaps three kilometres below Saint-Jérôme on the huge flatlands below the Alpilles, has an immense expanse beyond the house, formerly a pasture where the bulls and horses grazed. Its boundaries are a kilometre away to the south, with a low charcoal line of wooded ridge visible, the last outcrop of limestone before the Crau and the Camargue. Standing on her terrace, one's eye seems to wander outwards from the deep green of a formal maze immediately below, with its darkly delineated shapes, and then over a veritable sea of lavender beyond, undulating like waves in the wind and receding to a mist at the low line of the horizon. In the foreground at the side of the house is an ancient copse of tall, deciduous trees with the atmosphere of *Déjeuner sur l'Herbe*, graceful and monumental, uncluttered

by the woolly character of *pinède* and *maquis*. Although the two domains present an antithesis when one evokes the eye's wandering over gardens within contrasting landscapes, they seem bound together, both geologically (whatever their surface contour and clothing), and in the sense one has of a long history of cultivation from Celto-Ligurian times. The planting of an olive orchard on this flatland carries thoughts of fidelity to the tradition of the ancient Greeks who brought the olive to our region twenty-six centuries ago. Who knows? It is more than probable that such an orchard existed at this very spot before the devastating frost of 1789, with either a domestic *pressoir*, or the use of the huge one in the neighbouring Mas de la Dame. The only twinge of envy I sometimes have, accompanying my joy in the inspiring project of my new neighbour, is for her distant, flowing horizon. Whereas at Saint-Jérôme we savour being enclosed by a dramatic skyline, they have a calm wide view. It revives in my memory the remark of our old friend, the Mexican poet Octavio Paz, when he quoted to me two lines of Stephen's as among the great in the English language:

> *Eye, gazelle, delicate wanderer.*
> *Drinker of horizon's fluid line.*

Naturally, the ingathering of Paradise Dwellers from the north is characterized also by their love of the traditional Provençal planting: irises under olive trees; the veiling of retaining walls on the steep slopes by creeping rosemary; the statuesque yuccas and tender, feathery mimosas; the deep gloss of free-standing *Magnolia grandiflora*; above all, the inky-dark, undulating backdrop of the cypress windbreaks. The never-ending adventure is to marry all this indigenous character belonging to the landscape itself with the great range of plants which, it is felt, OUGHT to belong in this habitat. It is this compelling interest which guides the newcomers to the farmhouse style of the *mas*, rather than the more gloomy formality of the *pavillon* or *château*, where the gardens of geometric parterres are an extension of the architecture, imposing rules and lines which fetter the imagination of the plantsman.

For the most part there is more imaginative sharing of plantsmanship between the Paradise Dwellers than there is among the Seekers, for they care for history and for the natural vegetation of related landscapes. With their love of indigenous species, and of those traditionally cultivated in the region, they discover through experience a pattern of suitability to our limestone landscape for those plants which come from further afield; for instance, those which are bred from originally Chinese species seem to like us better than those from Japan. This is particularly true of paeonies. Mexican and Californian plants do well (except, of course, for lupins); among them choisya, ceanothus, carpenteria, zauschneria, eschscholzia.

However far afield memory and imagination may wander in the process of choosing plants according to the affinity of their natural habitat with one's own landscape, for the Paradise Dweller such imaginary voyages do not induce restlessness. On the contrary, the garden endows upon the spirit a feeling of repose and timelessness, so that one is inspired not only to look reflectively, but to walk, to read books, to listen to music, or the music of birdsong, in a mood of renewal and acceptance. As the senses are refreshed, so too is sensibility.

Once, when we arrived from our crowded London life and a tiring though pleasurable journey motoring through Burgundy, Stephen wrote in his diary:

March 31ˢᵗ

Perfectly still calm weather, still winter but with spring flooding in like a current of warm water into a cold, still pool – in a way then, autumnal like those days of late September, also very still, when a current of cold air foretelling winter flows in. Those autumnal days are like ripe life into which a faint stream of death flows, and these are like a still pool of death into which life flows. The stillness is the extraordinary thing, as though nature were anaesthetized, paralysed, receiving an injection from a needle. And, because of this, one has a feeling of acceptance, standing in the utterly still garden, as though the clear-as-crystal light of such a day loosened all one's ties with life, put one in a passive mood of acceptance. I could give up everything and just stay here for ever. The feeling is one of happiness – a great treasure chest or barn full of happiness which makes everything but this mood of identification with the still scene to be a burden to be put down – cast aside.

But with the change of weather a few days later he continued:

After the first two perfectly calm crystalline days, there was rain or grey skies, and when there were not these right till my last day which was lovely, there was mistral. I can't decide whether I love or hate the mistral; the point is that it seems to demand an attitude, a response from you, it does not leave you alone. Sometimes at night it makes our house creak and groan like a ship at sea in a gale. Daytimes the sky is clear. Bending the 'Cannes de Provence' at the edge of our garden the mistral makes the boughs of the olive trees in the orchard gleam like glass fibres; and below the orchard the rocks of the mountains seem like ridges carved in agate, polished as though under water.

The tirelessness of the mistral is itself tiring, like children who won't stop screaming, or a guest who outstays his welcome. It never stops reminding you, 'I made all this, I scooped out the rocks into folds, fans, scallop shells, ridges; I make the trees bend over so far that when I'm gone they never quite spring back again to the upright. I washed out the sky so that its pure blue is seen through a filter of dust, and the few white clouds are torn to shreds and tatters.'

The next passage from his diary of that visit puts me in mind of our long and cherished friendship with Henry and Irina Moore, from whom I learned so much about gardening. They shared a kind of mutual sensibility for the eternal and the seemingly ephemeral in nature, the forms inherent in rocks and stones – and then, the transformations in texture, in the tapestry of foliage, which carry a different sense of eternity in the rhythms of the seasons. Stephen wrote:

The time alone with N. was beautiful – with that kind of poignancy I feel about Saint-Jérôme because of N.'s passionate wrestling with the garden. I realized for the first time what a creative achievement a garden is, if it is one (or perhaps two) person's passion. A gardener is struggling with material like a sculptor with marble to make a statue. The gardener differs from the sculptor though, in that the sculptor completely imposes his will on the form. Or, if he views the form as implicit in the stone from which he is bringing it to birth, then he acts as midwife to the potentially formed. But the gardener is conducting a kind of dialogue with nature. Natasha offers plants to our stony, limey soil – some it accepts, some it rejects. It answers back and is a very living kind of thing.

He might have added that the art of pruning, though superficially akin to the sculptor's woodcarving, or even the skill of the hairdresser, is also tempered by one's solicitude for a living being; the gardener is always preoccupied by concern for health and wellbeing, so that the garden is not only studio but nursery.

We had visited Henry and Irina when they first moved to Hoglands at Much Hadham in Hertfordshire during the war, and we saw their garden evolve from the tiny area

*The 'knife-edge forms' photographed
by Stephen for Henry Moore*

*Previous page: Stephen and I celebrating our
Golden Wedding*

surrounding the house to the natural, gently curving walks through which one strolls today. The perfection of siting for each of the strong forms of the sculpture within the accommodating serenity of the garden speaks of an affectionate collaboration between Henry and Irina within their close marriage. They explained to us how Henry chose and placed the trees. He preferred the native species, creating the structural forms of the island beds which shaped the yielding masses of leaves forever in motion (the fluttering white poplars or the pendulous willows sweeping to the ground), to enhance, but never to war with, the great bronzes. Irina chose the planting of shrubs and perennials. She loved each individually, and used to talk with an amused affection of their choosing sometimes to grow in a manner she had not foreseen. She had an extraordinary feeling for the textures and gentle variety of foliage which led the eye onward down the path to the next moment of impact as one approached, for instance, a towering *Interlocking Form*. The close life of their creating the garden, Henry contributing the strong masculine element and Irina intuitively echoing his more malleable forms in the vegetation, was inspiring.

They had always wanted to come to Saint-Jérôme, but were invariably disappointed, almost enslaved to the deadlines dictating the day by which the latest commissioned work must be finished, to be borne away from studio or garden. But Henry kept and greatly enjoyed the photographs we gave him of our limestone ridge, the natural drama of the great near-vertical slabs, the slow, jagged incline of the rocks toward the main peak. In all our gardening gossip with them both concerning our choice of species, we always knew that they imagined the landscape truly as it is, and were the friends whose suggestions came from a consummate understanding of the relationship between implacable mineral forms and the sculptured, skeletal trees clothed each in its distinctive foliage.

I knew that when Stephen looked at the garden it was always with a painter's eye, yet the constant seductive interplay of colour was only a part of the whole. The sense of creating living sculpture within the circle of limestone forms carved over the ages by the arrogant mistral was something which we shared. Paradoxically, this sense seemed to have always been present in our imagination, to have inspired our first attraction to the place, and yet also to have been evolving rather slowly with the years. Stephen would stand at the window of his study, sketching always the same contours of rocks with the mounds of garden shrubs below as if, like repeating through a lifetime a poem or a piece of music, he would never come to the end in absorbing its beauty. There were a few such visual themes which perennially possessed his imagination over the years – a cave on the beach at Rovinia in Corfu, a distant hilltop in Tuscany – but most of all, the rocks and garden of Saint-Jérôme.

But there was yet another affinity between Henry and Stephen which chimed with the feeling for nature which enveloped us at Saint-Jérôme: that of a great sensibility for the relation of human or animal form to the more gentle lie of the land. It is apparent in Henry's works of genius, and its spontaneous expression in some landscape poems of Stephen's often fills my mind when I pause for a moment in my gardening to drink in the view. Through the years it has refined the way that I have imagined the garden ideally should reflect the landscape, though of course I wonder how far that ideal is ultimately attainable.

Contemplating a Moore sculpture which seemed 'part animal, part human, part rock face', Stephen said that in his best work Henry transformed primitive unconscious material (the stuff of dreams) into a 'shared consciousness of the profoundly human'. He was not primarily concerned with pleasing the senses, but more with a spiritual vitality which goes deeper than the senses, to which his lifelong devotion to Michelangelo bears witness. This sense of a profound energy released into form surrounds us in the Alpilles, where erosion is the artist, fashioning the pinnacles into hostile birds of prey or hunched bovine forms which speak of animal power. Yet the mounds of pasture or *pinède* which clothe the unreleased skeletons of rock below the surface evoke a more reposeful sense of reclining animal or human forms, where their power is latent rather than apparent. It is natural to wish to draw these timeless shapes into the modest living area of our two short human lives, a small, imperfect signature existing fleetingly upon an eternal landscape. How fortunate one is to be lent for a short span this tiny territory in which, in spite of all the botched beginnings, one can shape and encourage a family of beautiful plants to enjoy their existence.

The trophies of antiquity which surround us in this Greco-Roman outpost of a land touch us as a link to similarly modest lives of centuries ago, in the great surge which is the human race. I like to think of those people tending their olives, planting their flowers, gossiping with neighbours, drinking the local wine, much as we do. And, doubtless, their sense of their puny though energetic endeavours as being minimal within the power of nature, personified in their gods, was fundamentally little different from our own. A century or two hence there may remain vestiges of our garden in surviving trees, and passers-by will be seized, as we were, by the magic of the site and its power to release one from the disenchantment of daily life, 'getting and spending and laying waste our powers' in a large metropolis. Then it will be for them as it is for us, as if the rhythm of the natural world surrounding us here imposes its own tempo upon our thoughts, which become attuned to it and thus liberated into a pace which gives those thoughts freedom and clarity.

As for ourselves, we have always been at our happiest in this peaceful life of making – whether it be a poem or a garden – always most alive when the sense of leaving a minute mark upon the grandeur of an eternal landscape is the true reality and consolation. When I pause and gaze, in the midst of early morning watering or weeding, it is often these lines of Stephen's, written 'In Attica', that other antique Mediterranean land of contours, which float into my memory.

Again, again, I see this form repeated:
The bare shadow of a rock outlined
Against the sky; declining gently to
An elbow; then the scooped descent
From the elbow to the wrist of a hand that rests
On the plain.
              Again, again,
That arm outstretched from the high shoulder
And leaning on the land.
                    As though the torsoed
Gods, with heads and lower limbs broken off
Plunged in the sky, or buried under earth,
Had yet left arms extended here as pointers
Between the sun and plain:
                      had made this landscape
Human, like Greek steles, where the dying
Are changed to stone on a gesture of curved air
Lingering in their infinite departure.

Acknowledgements

Some years back, with little evidence of my aptitude for the task, Christopher MacLehose bravely suggested that I write this book for Harvill. His colleague at the time, Mark Bonham-Carter followed up with a blend of friendly encouragement and exhortation. I owe them both a great debt of gratitude for their patience, and for a faith which was often greater than my own. Friends in England, Jane Astor, Lindy Dufferin, Tim Rees, Eunice Robinson, have helped with sharing enjoyable expeditions, taking photographs, or making horticultural suggestions. Ed and Carol Victor and Nigel Nicolson gave unforgettable hospitality at Sissinghurst.

In Provence, many friends contributed local expertise and generous hospitality: The Right Honourable Ann Cox Chambers at Le Petit Fontanille, Anne Dunn (Moynihan) and Francis Wishart at Le Domaine de Saint-Estève, Nicolas and Dorothy Kroll at Les Quatres Sources, Yves Coutarel and Robert Parkinson at the Rue de l'Amoureux in Tarascon. Georges Grillet instructed me in exotics, with guided tours of the municipal hothouses of Tarascon. The late Christopher Cornford presented me with the drawing that features as endpapers, which he had made perched perilously on a chair atop a table on the brink of the steps to the olive orchard. Iris and John Bayley read chapter one and encouraged me, commenting gleefully on fastigiate tree-forms in stone.

My editor, Sophie Henley-Price, has been resourceful in picture research, patient in seeing the book through technical stages, and unfailingly cheerful.

Glossary of French terms

Acte de Vente — sale agreement
aigres-doux — bitter-sweet
arcade — arch
atelier — workshop

Bambouserie — bamboo nursery
bassin — pool, tank
bergerie — sheep-pen
bigarreaux — white-heart cherry
boule (acacia boule) — bushy-topped tree; here round-shaped acacia
boules — the game of bowls
burlats — large, firm, dark red cherry

Canisse — long, thin canes used as a protecting hedge in Provence
cannes de Provence — plant resembling a coarse bamboo, used for making screens and windbreaks
cers Languedocien — wind of the Languedoc
chevalet — A-shaped wooden ladder for fruit-picking
confiserie — confectionery
confiture — preserve; jam
coulis (de tomates) — (tomato) sauce
cuisine — cooking

Demi-lune — half-moon
département — Department; sub-division of France
doyen — senior exponent

droit de puisage — the right to draw water from a well

Engrais — fertilizer
esprit de corps — esprit de corps; corporate feeling
étang — pond
expéditeur — confiner of goods

Fromage blanc — fresh, creamy white cheese

Garrigue — stony, sun drenched hills, with sparse vegetation
géomètre — surveyor
gourmands — suckers
griotte — Morello cherry

Increvable — drought-proof, indestructible

Les grandes chaleurs — the hottest part of the summer

Maquis — maquis, scrub
mas — Provençal farmhouse
métier — profession
mirabelle — small plum

Olives cassées — olives, lightly crushed and soaked in lye to remove the bitterness whilst retaining the texture of a raw olive

Panniers — baskets
patois — (provincial) dialect
patron — boss
paysage — landscape
pépiniériste — nurseryman
pierre apparente — exposed stonework, unrendered
pierre de Fontvieille — stone coming from Fontvieille
pierre de Rognes — stone coming from Rognes
pinède — pine forest
poche d'eau — water pocket
potager — kitchen garden
pression à froid — cold-pressing
pressoir — oil-press

Récolte — harvest
rentable — profitable
romaines — Roman-style tiles

Sondages — soundings
serres — glasshouses

Terrain — plot of land
terreau — compost
tramontane de Roussillon — north wind in Roussillon

Vigne vierge — Virginia creeper

Index of plants

Photography

First published in 1999 by
The Harvill Press
2 Aztec Row, Berners Road
London N1 0PW

www.harvill-press.com

Text copyright © Natasha Spender 1999

Natasha Spender asserts her moral right to be identified as the author of this work

A CIP catalogue record for this book is available from the British Library

ISBN 1 86046 514 5

Designed by Clive Crook. Assisted by Yvonne Cash. Set in 10.5pt Caslon
Originated, printed and bound in Italy by Conti Tipocolor, Florence